Mr John

John Cobbold: The Most Eccentric Man In Football Ever

KNOW THE SCORE BOOKS SPORTS PUBLICATIONS

CULT HEROES	Author	*ISBN*
CARLISLE UNITED	Paul Harrison	978-1-905449-09-7
CELTIC	David Potter	978-1-905449-08-8
CHELSEA	Leo Moynihan	1-905449-00-3
MANCHESTER CITY	David Clayton	978-1-905449-05-7
NEWCASTLE	Dylan Younger	1-905449-03-8
NOTTINGHAM FOREST	David McVay	978-1-905449-06-4
RANGERS	Paul Smith	978-1-905449-07-1
SOUTHAMPTON	Jeremy Wilson	1-905449-01-1
WEST BROM	Simon Wright	1-905449-02-X

MATCH OF MY LIFE	Editor	*ISBN*
BRIGHTON	Paul Camillin	978-1-84818-000-0
DERBY COUNTY	Nick Johnson	978-1-905449-68-2
ENGLAND WORLD CUP	Massarella & Moynihan	1-905449-52-6
EUROPEAN CUP FINALS	Ben Lyttleton	1-905449-57-7
FA CUP FINALS 1953-1969	David Saffer	978-1-905449-53-8
FULHAM	Michael Heatley	1-905449-51-8
IPSWICH TOWN	Mel Henderson	978-1-84818-001-7
LEEDS	David Saffer	1-905449-54-2
LIVERPOOL	Leo Moynihan	1-905449-50-X
MANCHESTER UNITED	Ivan Ponting	978-1-905449-59-0
SHEFFIELD UNITED	Nick Johnson	1-905449-62-3
STOKE CITY	Simon Lowe	978-1-905449-55-2
SUNDERLAND	Rob Mason	1-905449-60-7
WOLVES	Simon Lowe	1-905449-56-9

PLAYER BY PLAYER	Author	*ISBN*
LIVERPOOL	Ivan Ponting	978-1-84818-306-3
MANCHESTER UNITED	Ivan Ponting	978-1-84818-500-1
TOTTENHAM HOTSPUR	Ivan Ponting	978-1-84818-501-8

GREATEST GAMES	Author	*ISBN*
SCOTLAND	David Potter	978-1-84818-200-4
STOKE CITY	Simon Lowe & David Lee	978-1-84818-201-1
WEST BROM	Simon Wright	978-1-84818-206-6

GENERAL FOOTBALL	Author	ISBN
A GREAT FACE FOR RADIO	John Anderson	978-1-84818-403-9
A SMASHING LITTLE FOOTBALL FIRM	Nicky Allt	978-1-84818-402-2
BEHIND THE BACK PAGE	Christopher Davies	978-1-84818-506-7
BOOK OF FOOTBALL OBITUARIES	Ivan Ponting	978-1-905449-82-2
FORGIVE US OUR PRESS PASSES	Football Writers' Association	978-1-84818-507-4
JUST ONE OF SEVEN	Denis Smith	978-1-84818-504-3
MANCHESTER UNITED MAN & BABE	Wilf McGuinness	978-1-84818-503-6
NEVER HAD IT SO GOOD	Tim Quelch	978-1-84818-600-2
NO SMOKE, NO FIRE	Dave Jones	978-1-84818-513-5
NORTHERN AND PROUD	Paul Harrison	978-1-84818-505-0
OUTCASTS: The Lands That FIFA Forgot	Steve Menary	978-1-905449-31-6
PALLY	Gary Pallister	978-1-84818-500-5
PARISH TO PLANET	Eric Midwinter	978-1-905449-30-9
PLEASE MAY I HAVE MY FOOTBALL BACK?	Eric Alexander	978-1-84818-508-1
TACKLES LIKE A FERRET	Paul Parker	1-905449-46-1
THE DOOG	Harrison & Gordos	978-1-84818-502-9
THE RIVALS GAME	Douglas Beattie	978-1-905449-79-8
UNITED NATIONS?	Tim Webber	978-1-84818-405-3
WARK ON	John Wark	978-1-84818-511-1

RUGBY LEAGUE	Author	ISBN
MOML LEEDS RHINOS	Caplan & Saffer	978-1-905449-69-9
MOML WIGAN WARRIORS	David Kuzio	978-1-905449-66-8

CRICKET	Author	ISBN
ASHES TO DUST	Graham Cookson	978-1-905449-19-4
GROVEL!	David Tossell	978-1-905449-43-9
KP: CRICKET GENIUS?	Wayne Veysey	978-1-84818-701-6
MOML: THE ASHES	Pilger & Wightman	1-905449-63-1
MY TURN TO SPIN	Shaun Udal	978-1-905449-42-2
THE BEST OF ENEMIES	Kidd & McGuinness	978-1-84818-703-1
THE BODYLINE HYPOCRISY	Michael Arnold	978-1-84818-702-3
WASTED?	Paul Smith	978-1-905449-45-3

John Cobbold: The Most Eccentric Man In Football Ever

Mel Henderson
Foreword by Allan Hunter

www.knowthescorebooks.com

First published in the United Kingdom
by Know The Score Books Ltd, 2009

© and ® Know The Score Books Limited. All rights reserved 2009.

The right of Mel Henderson to be identified as the author of this work has been asserted by him in accordance with sections 77 and 78 of the Copyright, Designs and Patents Act, 1988.

Know The Score Books Limited
118 Alcester Road, Studley, Warwickshire, B80 7NT
01527 454482
info@knowthescorebooks.com
www.knowthescorebooks.com

A CIP catalogue record is available for this book from the British Library
ISBN: 978-1-84818-514-2

Jacket design by Graham Hales

Printed and bound in Great Britain by Athaeneum Press, Gateshead, Tyne & Wear

Photographs copyright Getty Images, Owen Hines, Dave Kindred, Ipswich Town FC. Cover photograph copyright Archant.

Contents

ACKNOWLEDGEMENTS

Apart from those only too willing to rewind and remember the good times they experienced in the company of John Cobbold, I would like to place on record my grateful thanks to Mr John for providing me with a host of happy memories and the inspiration to put them in book form. His untimely death meant that his intended autobiography, ghosted by yours truly, was never published; may this book go some way to filling that unfortunate void.

I am extremely grateful to Debbie Noye, who was my secretary at the time, for her original transcription of Mr John's tapes, while thanks must also go to Simon Lowe and his staff at Know the Score Books for their encouragement, assistance and support. To see my efforts, together with Mr John's own story in his own words for the very first time, in print feels like a debt at long last repaid to someone who opened my eyes and inspired me long after our time together had expired. My life was considerably enriched for having known the kind, generous and, it has to be said, often outrageous Mr John.

Mel Henderson, October 2009

*"People have asked what we are
going to do with the sponsors' money.
We intend to spend some on wine, women and song,
and we shall probably squander the rest."*

Mr John Cobbold

Foreword
by Allan Hunter

WHEN I WAS transferred from Blackburn Rovers to Ipswich Town in September 1971 I made a point of going along to Ewood Park to say my farewells and something the chairman told me was still fresh in my mind when I arrived at Portman Road the next day. He said, "Allan, I don't know much about the football club, but you're going to a hell of a chairman." I wondered what he meant, but didn't have long to find out. My wife, Carol, and my young son, Lee, who was approaching his second birthday, were with me just outside the club offices when a car – I remember it was a Rover – made its way down the long drive from the main entrance. As it approached we could see someone was standing up with the top half of his body outside the sun roof and when it pulled up close to us the person was pretending that he had a rifle in his hands and was 'shooting' at us and in particular Lee. Seconds later he jumped out and introduced himself.

I shall never forget that first meeting with Mr John and how the words of his Blackburn counterpart, which had initially puzzled me, suddenly made perfect sense. If I feel proud to have played for Ipswich – I had 11 mainly happy years with the club – my life was certainly enriched for knowing Mr John. I have never met, and probably never will meet, a nicer human being. He always had a smile on his face and I can picture him now with that infectious laugh of his as he cracked a joke or told an amusing anecdote. Life was certainly never dull with Mr John around.

We shared many an adventure together. When he discovered that we were both born on 30 June, albeit 19 years apart, he christened me 'brother' and 'twin' and for several years he sent me a birthday card to mark the occasion. When we met he would greet me, as only Mr John could, with a swear word or two and I recall an occasion when Ipswich were playing Norwich at Portman Road and I could have had him arrested. Officers from the Norfolk Constabulary were drafted in to help deal with any trouble between rival fans and they were congregated under one of the stands as I made my way back to the dressing room area from the club's Centre Spot restaurant, where we had enjoyed our pre-match meal. Mr John was also nearby, dressed in his tweed outfit of jacket and plus fours, complete with a massive hole in one of his long socks, and when he spotted me he let out a cry: "Hello, you big Irish bastard!" One of the policemen from Norfolk was quick to ask me, "Shall I sort that bloke out for you?" and when I replied, "That's our chairman," the copper's face was a picture as he blurted out the words, "You're kidding?"

I had only been an Ipswich player for a short period when the club announced they were taking us off to Magaluf in Majorca for a few days. The manager, Bobby Robson, said it would be an ideal opportunity for me to get to know my colleagues better but my abiding memory of the trip is how I slung a very drunk Mr John over my shoulder and carried him to his bedroom, only for him to surface on a further two occasions and for me to do exactly the same all over again. He loved a drink and it was on that trip that I recall how he sat down at breakfast with a bottle of dry white wine and some dry toast.

Mr John was very well connected, of course, and one of the few occasions I saw him in the Ipswich dressing room was when he brought in the Prime Minister at the time, Ted Heath, to meet the players before a game. Ted had that trademark laugh of his, with his shoulders going up and down, and as he did it what he didn't know was that Mr John was right behind him mimicking him. Of course, his uncle was Harold Macmillan, another former Prime Minister, and I recall Mr John telling me an amusing tale. He said he was intending to host a surprise party for Mama, a term he always used when referring to his mother, Lady Blanche. He was a bit tipsy as he explained in his Old Etonian accent that he had written to a number of family members, including Harold Macmillan, to invite them to attend. He said, "The silly old bugger, Uncle Harold has only written back to Mama and told her he is very sorry but he will not be able to attend her surprise party. No wonder this country's in such a mess." Mr John seemed to know so many people from so many different walks of life. For example, on my very first away trip with Ipswich – we were playing West Bromwich Albion the next day – I was walking through the hotel after dinner when Mr John caught sight of me and invited me to join him and his companion, who turned out to be none other than the comedian, Arthur Askey.

The accusation: 'He couldn't organise a piss-up in a brewery' could never have been levelled at Mr John. Not only did he own a brewery, he had literally hundreds of pubs. There was a time in my playing career when I started to think ahead to what I might do when the time came to hang up my boots and I decided it might be an idea to be a pub landlord. Not a very original idea, perhaps, but when Mr John caught wind of the fact he came to me and said, "Pick whatever pub you want and it will be yours." I have no doubt that he meant it but as things turned out I changed my mind, put off by the fact that I could see myself working seven days a week. He had a tremendous sense of fun and liked nothing better than a practical joke. We were staying in a hotel up north after a match and Bobby Robson drummed it in to us that we had to be on time for the bus the next morning. More than once he reminded us about the departure time, adding, "If you're not there we will go without you." Come the morning, everyone was on the coach except the manager, who had been sidetracked. We waited for a few minutes before Mr John ordered the driver to move off slowly and I shall never forget the sight of the manager running across the car park just in time to hop on board, at which point he was greeted by the chairman laughing out loud.

It was when I went off to represent my country that I realised how fortunate I was to be playing for Ipswich and to have someone like Mr John in charge. My Northern Ireland colleagues couldn't believe some of the stories I told them. They were jealous of the fact that I was even on speaking terms with the chairman because at their clubs most of them had never even encountered the man at the top, never mind spent time in his company enjoying a laugh and a few drinks. Our trips into Europe, which were more frequent as the club became more successful, and end-of-season jaunts to faraway places like Barbados and Martinique, were right up Mr John's street. We usually set off on a Monday when we were playing the away leg of a European tie and Mr John would think nothing of buying the players a round of drinks the minute we were airborne. This was something Bobby Robson had no intention of encouraging and he had no choice but to put his foot down and insist that Mr John waited until after we had played the game before he got the drinks in. Bobby even allocated himself a seat on the plane behind everyone else so that he could see what was going on and make sure the chairman behaved himself.

There was one classic occasion when Mr John acted as peacemaker between the manager and I. Bobby got us together in the dressing room one day and said he was planning a mid-season trip to Israel. I listened to what he had to say before telling him there was no way I would be travelling, not with the Golan Heights conflict on-going. Bobby said, "You would go to Belfast, would you not?" and I replied, "Yes, but I know my way round there." He wasn't amused when David Johnson piped up, "If the Big Man isn't going then neither am I," but we were the only two who raised any objection.

We had an away game at Leeds immediately before the Israel trip and the plan was that the team bus would head straight down the M1 to Heathrow. That meant that Jonty and I had to find a way of returning to Ipswich and the club secretary, David Rose, agreed he would drive us back. It was half-time and we were sitting in the dressing room at Elland Road, with the manager delivering his team talk, when there was a knock on the door. He ignored it and carried on but the person knocked again. Once more the manager disregarded it but when the person on the other side of the door persisted he eventually relented and turned to Cyril Lea, the first-team coach, to ask, "Would you mind getting that?" Cyril opened the door and the chap who stood there said, "Message for Mr Robson," as he thrust a piece of paper into Cyril's hand. Cyril handed it over, Bobby read it and immediately turned to me. "You'll be happy," he said, "because the Israel trip has just been cancelled." At the end of the game, therefore, Jonty and I jumped on the bus that was now heading back to Ipswich but we could see Bobby was far from happy. A regular stop on return trips to Ipswich was the George Hotel in Stamford and we were lucky that when they were contacted by phone, and asked if a party of about 20 people could book in for dinner, they were able to accommodate us. When we had finished our main course everyone but for Jonty and I departed the dining room. We both decided we wanted a sweet – I had a crème caramel and he ordered strawberries. We were tucking into our desserts when Bobby came back into the dining room with a face like thunder. The nearest member of staff was a young girl in full waitress uniform and she looked a bit surprised when Bobby pointed to Jonty's bowl and said, "Miss, where are these strawberries from?" She went to check and came back with the information that they were from Spain, at which point Bobby turned to Jonty and said, "It's a good job they're not from Israel or you would be in trouble." At that Jonty absolutely flipped. We were sitting at one end of a long table and at the other end there was a huge log fire. Jonty threw his dish of strawberries along the table and it skidded several feet before the whole lot landed in the fireplace. The waitress disappeared quickly to the safety of the kitchen, Bobby turned on his heels and left, and once he'd gone Jonty and I headed straight for the bar and ordered two pints. The rest of the lads were on the bus and word reached us that if we didn't hurry up and join them we would be left behind. When we got to the bus we went towards the back and sat down. We had a television set on the bus and as we set off on the last leg of our journey *Match of the Day* was just starting. Back then Bobby featured in the opening credits, with a shot of him sitting on the bench in his sheepskin coat. When he appeared I shouted, "Israel, Israel." He reacted angrily, leaping off his seat and marching towards the back of the bus to confront me. I stood up to face him and before it had a chance to turn ugly Mr John appeared on the scene. "Come on Bobby," he said, "get back to the front of the bus and learn to have a sense of humour." That was the end of the matter.

Mr John used to take all his laundry to a dry cleaning business in Felixstowe and I remember him furiously scratching round his neck one day. "They've put too much bloody starch on my shirt collar," he complained. Apparently they had also starched his pyjamas and it wasn't long before he took his business elsewhere. Talking of pyjamas, we saw rather a lot of him in his bedtime attire. He would invite everyone from the club to his home at Capel Hall for a pre-season party. Weather permitting, it would start in his impressive grounds but later in the evening it would continue indoors. I remember one night when my wife and I, together with goalkeeper Laurie Sivell and his wife, were the only guests remaining. Mr John decided to turn in for the night, apologised and went upstairs. But he later returned in his striped pyjamas, commenting, "Are you fuckers still here?" Then he proceeded to crack open another bottle before once again retreating to bed, but not before he reminded us to switch off the lights and lock up when we eventually went home. My wife, Carol, also remembers how she and one or two of the other wives were coming downstairs as Mr John was going up and he didn't flinch as he commented, "Been for a piss, girls?"

A natural comedian, Mr John was also an accomplished pianist and there were a number of occasions when I heard him play. He liked nothing better than to play and for the players to join him, gathering round the piano for a sing-song. I recall one particular occasion, when we were preparing for a new season with a training trip to Holland, and his playing was received very enthusiastically by our fellow guests in the hotel dining room. Players, coaches and managers are always talking about team spirit and the vital part it can play in a club's success. We had it in abundance during my time at Ipswich and while I would never underestimate the manager's part, I would have to say that Mr John's style of chairmanship was another huge factor in generating a tremendous working environment, one that was the envy of players at many other clubs. We all knew we were blessed with probably the best chairman of all time and appreciated it.

In 1982, when my time was up at Portman Road and I was heading off to become player-manager at Colchester, he took me up to the boardroom and opened a bottle of champagne. Then another. He thanked me for the part I had played in the club's success and we sat there for a couple of hours reflecting on events of the previous 11 years. Even as he clung to life in September 1983 he had a smile on his face and that wicked sense of humour was working overtime. I had written to him after learning he was ill and he replied to invite me to go over to Capel Hall and see him. At the very bottom of the letter, in handwriting clearly different to his own, someone – possibly his chauffeur, Roger – had written the words 'Make it soon.' I wasted no time in driving over to the house – Roger Osborne accompanied me – and we were shown up to his bedroom, where he had a nurse on full-time watch. Of course, given the gravity of his illness, it wasn't the Mr John I had known. At least, not physically, because I was immediately struck by the amount of weight he had shed. But mentally he was still very alert. We each had a cigarette and the nurse said that by the time he had finished his he would be close to falling asleep. I remember his brother, Patrick, entered the room and, not realising he was still awake, asked the nurse how he was. Before the nurse had an opportunity to reply Mr John found the strength to speak and said, "I'm still here. You won't be getting your hands on my fucking money just yet." Seconds later he was fast asleep, at which point Roger and I left. We were informed the very next day of his death.

I'll admit to being a bit eccentric myself – some people just think me downright odd – and maybe that was why Mr John and I hit it off so well.

It would take a far better man than me to do him justice, but to describe him as eccentric is only half the story. He was incredibly generous, to the extent that Ipswich was the only club where drinks in both the guest room and the players' lounge were complimentary. We were used to paying for drinks in the players' lounges at the other clubs but when it was suggested that Ipswich should adopt a similar policy Mr John simply would not hear of it. The club was renowned for its hospitality, particularly during his period as chairman. Mr John was at home in any company, not just when he was surrounded by members of the royal family, many of whom were personal friends and whose company he enjoyed during weekend shoots held on his own patch of Suffolk. He was no snob and I like the story of him standing at the brewery gates with members of staff who were on strike. There he was, not just sympathetic to their cause, but warming his hands on the brazier as he chatted away. I can't speak for all the others who came across Mr John but I am in no doubt that he was by far the nicest person I ever met.

Allan Hunter

Allan Hunter is Ipswich Town's most capped international player, representing Northern Ireland on 47 occasions – many of them as captain – during his time at Portman Road and winning a total of 53 caps alongside giants of the British game like Pat Jennings and George Best. Previously with Coleraine, Oldham Athletic and Blackburn Rovers, he made 355 appearances for Ipswich and scored 10 goals. He was a member of the side that won the FA Cup in 1978. A defensive tower of strength, he has been named as one of the club's top ten stars of all time and supporters voted him their Player of the Year in 1976.

Introduction
by Mel Henderson

THE HUGE OUTPOURING of grief the length and breadth of England – and well beyond these shores – following news of Sir Bobby Robson's death on 31 July 2009 was exactly what one would have expected. Rarely has the football community been so united in paying its respects, with supporters setting aside club rivalries and instead joining forces to honour someone who had long since been regarded as a national treasure. Not only did they enthusiastically embrace the minute's applause before every side's first home league game of the new season, but the replica shirts of clubs north and south of the border that were positioned alongside floral tributes adjacent to his statue at Portman Road underlined how his popularity extended well beyond Suffolk, where he was, and will always remain, Ipswich's favourite son.

As Bobby consistently acknowledged, however, none of what he achieved in an outstanding managerial career would have been possible without the unstinting support of Ipswich chairman John Cobbold, the man who appointed him and backed him to the hilt during his 13 years and five months in charge at Portman Road. So close were they that Bobby always referred to him as being "like a second father to me," which was the ultimate compliment to an equally great and much-loved man. Mr John, as he was universally known, was different to other chairmen. Indeed, he was unique, as I sincerely hope this book will reveal.

He and Bobby were a double act, brought together early in 1969 by fate as preferred candidates Billy Bingham and Frank O'Farrell, who went on to manage Everton and Manchester United respectively, declined the opportunity to succeed Bill McGarry, who had resigned a few weeks earlier. McGarry was convinced that Wolverhampton Wanderers would offer him a greater chance of managerial fulfilment, only to discover that the very opposite was the case. But his decision, together with those of Messrs Bingham and O'Farrell, was to work to Ipswich's advantage. Bobby, out of work after being sacked by Fulham, the club he represented as a player both before and after his time with West Bromwich Albion, was so desperate for another chance that he agreed to take the job despite the reluctance of Mr John and his fellow directors to offer him a contract.

Soon, despite some minor hiccups, Bobby would realise he was working for the best chairman in the game, someone who would refuse to buckle when the going got tough, a trait he amply demonstrated in the wake of a comprehensive home defeat by Manchester United on 7 September 1971, by which time Bobby had been in charge for two years and eight months. Town lost 3-1 to the Old Trafford side in a League Cup second round tie, the main difference between the sides being a scintillating individual display by the one and only George Best, who scored twice to inspire his side to recover from the setback of Scottish star Jimmy Robertson's eighth minute opener.

A section of the crowd called for the manager's head and Bobby, only too aware of the fact that a board meeting was scheduled for the very next day, admitted he feared the worst when Mr John chose to remind him of it before departing the ground. Bobby even confessed that he returned home that evening and told his wife, Elsie, that she might as well start packing. The next morning, as he drove the short journey from his home in Capel St Mary to Portman Road, Bobby was in apprehensive mood, his knees trembling at the prospect of being returned to football's scrapheap as the latest in a long line of managerial casualties. But he was in for a shock as he took his seat alongside the directors in the boardroom. Mr John kicked off proceedings by apologising to the manager for some supporters' reaction the previous night, stated that should it happen again he would tender his own resignation and then, in a move unprecedented anywhere, virtually insisted that Bobby commit himself to a lengthy, ten-year contract in a show of solidarity that was to extend for more than a decade.

In that time, thanks to Ipswich's success, Bobby was much sought-after within the game. Not only in England, where Derby, Leeds, Manchester United, Sunderland and Everton were willing to meet whatever wage demands he made of them, but in Spain, where Athletic Bilbao and Barcelona also invited him to name his price. He could even have taken over the national side of Saudi Arabia, a role that may have lacked prestige but one that would have made him a millionaire overnight. Every time they came calling Mr John stood firm and repelled each raid. Even after Bobby met Everton's hierarchy at a motorway service station one Sunday afternoon and agreed to become the new manager at Goodison he found it impossible to sever his partnership with Mr John.

It was early in 1977 and Bobby came into Portman Road on a double mission – to tender his resignation and then clear out his desk. But an exclusive back page story in a national newspaper, which revealed the move, ultimately led to a change of heart. Bobby had insisted the deal should only be announced once he had dealt with his departure from Ipswich in the right and proper manner. He was appalled that the news had been leaked and immediately sought out Mr John to explain the situation. With tears in his eyes, Bobby admitted he had intended to quit but in a dramatic twist was now pleading to be allowed to stay, a request, of course, to which a much relieved Mr John was only too pleased to agree.

But Bobby's anger was such that he requested, as a personal favour, that I write a letter to Everton on his behalf. He explained that, having agreed to take the job as manager of the Toffees, he felt it would be only right to provide them with a written explanation for his sudden about-turn. Their generous offer included a £50,000 'signing-on' fee – Bobby showed me the cheque they had handed over less than 24 hours earlier – and they had also agreed to buy his house in Suffolk to enable him to relocate immediately to Merseyside. Bobby asked me to make the last paragraph of the letter a reference to the fact that he was returning the cheque and then, having approved its contents, he tore the cheque into confetti-sized pieces before 'pouring' it into the envelope addressed to Goodison Park.

Throughout a career that saw him become England boss in 1982, then manage abroad with PSV Eindhoven (Holland), Sporting Lisbon and Porto (Portugal) and Barcelona (Spain) before taking charge of his beloved Newcastle in September 1999, at the age of 66, he never missed an opportunity to thank his lucky stars for Ipswich, and in particular Mr John. He knew how much he owed him, not only for providing him with an opportunity to resurrect his career at the highest level but for steadfastly supporting him throughout his time at Portman Road, a period that forged his reputation as one of the greatest English managers of all time. 'He never wavered in his support for me,' wrote Bobby in his autobiography *Farewell but not Goodbye*, also adding, 'John was a truly terrific guy.'

I could not agree more, but the very first time I met John Cobbold might also have been the last. Instead, thankfully, I knew him for more than nine years until his untimely death in September 1983, when he was just 56. I recall how I had chatted to him at Ipswich Town's annual photo-call just a few weeks earlier, when he told me he had left four double-sided tapes on the desk in my office that was adjacent to Bobby's. "I'm off to see the quack," I remember him saying.

"Oh dear, nothing serious I hope?" I replied, at which point he insisted, "No, not at all, just a check-up." I never saw him again.

Sadly, he was told that very day that he had cancer of the spine, not disease of the liver as some had speculated would eventually prove his ruin, and after a brief stay in hospital he returned home to Capel Hall, his 2,000-acre estate at Kirton, near Felixstowe, where he passed away peacefully with younger brother Patrick at his bedside.

The tapes? They were recorded by him in the summer of 1983 after I suggested he should write his autobiography, an idea that clearly captured his imagination, although he only went along with it after I agreed to 'ghost' it for him. Of course, I had not even considered the possibility that he would be dead within a matter of weeks of putting his life story on tape. It must remain a mystery as to why he tackled the task with such haste. We will never know if he knew he was dying or whether it was purely coincidental.

My life, together with those of a great many people who crossed his path, no matter how briefly, was enriched for having known John Cobbold. The nine years I spent as Ipswich Town's public relations officer with him as chairman and director were an absolute joy; the tenth, in stark contrast, was like a chore by comparison as I saw the club start its downward spiral, like a rudderless ship, towards terminal decline with no-one seemingly capable of halting the slide.

My story starts in the summer of 1974. Soon after my return from the World Cup finals in West Germany, I was pleasantly surprised to be invited to Ipswich for an interview after I had applied for the job as the club's first-ever public relations officer, to which I was alerted by a tiny advertisement that leapt out from the sports pages of a national newspaper.

I was 23 and the sports editor of Scotland's largest weekly newspaper, *The Falkirk Herald*, and only my frustration at being told, on more than one occasion, that I lacked the necessary experience to join one of the Glasgow or Edinburgh-based national newspapers, led to me looking further afield for my next place of employment. I was actually pursuing two jobs simultaneously and my experience at Oxford United a few weeks earlier very nearly led to me withdrawing my application at Ipswich. The city of dreaming spires was also home to the ramshackle Manor Ground, where a chance meeting was to alter the course of my life.

Cramped and dilapidated, Oxford United's former home was a depressing sight as I entered. I paused to glance around then walked round the pitch to the opposite side, before locating the boardroom where interviews were already in session. I sat awaiting my turn in the company of another candidate, a local journalist whose name I have long since forgotten, and upon learning that he was bound for London later that day I suggested that I should accompany him on the first leg of my homeward journey, to which he immediately agreed.

My interview did not last long. I was asked if I had read the job description and whether I had any observations I wished to make. I made just one, referring the directors to the paragraph declaring 'the public relations officer will be expected to double the crowd' and expressed my dismay. "With all due respect," I told them, "there is only one man present here today who could realistically expect to succeed in that task – and that is the manager." Gerry Summers was his name and I never did find out what he thought of my remark, but I simply meant that a winning team, rather than any gimmicks in the shape of pre-match entertainment or whatever, would have the desired effect on crowds.

I left the room knowing that I was not going to be relocating to Oxford and on the train journey into London I happened to mention to my travelling companion that there seemed little point in following up my failure to impress at Oxford, then a Second Division club, by attending the interview at Ipswich, who had finished fourth in the First Division the previous season. "You have an interview at Ipswich?" he said, clearly envious. "I applied for that job and I don't have an interview," he continued. "Take my advice and don't cancel. They are a great club and they have the best chairman in the country."

I did heed his advice, but based on my experience of making the journey to and from Oxford by train – I booked a sleeper to head home to Glasgow and it turned out to be a 24-hour round trip – I wanted to avoid a repeat and decided to ask Ipswich Town, since they had already agreed to meet my travel expenses, if I could travel by air. "You will have to ask the chairman," I was told by a female voice at Portman Road, which I was to later identify as that of Pat Godbold, secretary to a succession of Town managers dating back to Scott Duncan and, I am pleased to say, someone who remains a friend to this day. Pat provided me with the number of the Tolly Cobbold brewery and I rang straight away. I asked to speak to John Cobbold, was successfully put through and after introducing myself I asked if it would be okay to travel by plane. "I really don't mind how you fucking well get here," he said. "I look forward to meeting you next week." And with that the line went dead.

Had I not had the 'best chairman in the country' words of the chap from Oxford ringing in my ears I might have been put off by such a blunt response, perhaps even to the extent of cancelling my interview. However, I subsequently made the journey to London by air, transferred to Ipswich by rail and upon entering the ground at around 4pm I was escorted into the boardroom by Pat.

A cheery, red-faced character met me, shook me warmly by the hand and said he was the chairman. So this was Mr John. "Would you like a drink?" he asked, and I, for reasons that 35 years later remain strangely vague, replied, "Yes please, can I have a Scotch?" Those who know me will vouch for the fact that I am not much of a drinker, especially of my home country's most successful export, so I have absolutely no explanation for my reaction. But Mr John certainly looked pleased and smiled as he said, "Thank fuck for that. We've been interviewing all day and no-one else has asked for a drink. Now we can all have one!" He then proceeded to throw open the doors of a cabinet in the corner, revealing all sorts of delights, and started to pour out drinks for his fellow directors. It did not escape my attention that Bobby declined – in fact he wore a look of utter condemnation – while the others participated with great enthusiasm.

The interview seemed to go well and within an hour I was heading back to the railway station to make the long trip home. A few days later Bobby rang me at home one evening and offered me the job, at which point I asked for a couple of days to mull it over with my wife. It really was a no-brainer, or it would have been had that phrase been around at the time, and

I rang back to confirm my acceptance before arranging to travel down to look at houses ahead of starting my new job in mid-September 1974.

I was booked into the Golden Lion Hotel and had only been there a few days when the phone rang in my room. "Hello Mel, John Cobbold here. What are you up to? How about popping over here for a few drinks and then we'll nip out for some lunch." I explained that I had just popped out to buy some newspapers and, since I was wearing an old jumper and jeans, would have to tidy myself up, at which point he said, "Nonsense, I'm wearing much the same. Just get yourself over here." I managed to find my way to Capel Hall, went round to the back of the house as instructed and found Mr John sitting there, gazing out over his own private piece of England, much of which was tended by tenant farmers.

"Help yourself to champagne," he said, nodding in the direction of the fridge in the kitchen. Then he carefully instructed me to be sure to replace the half bottle I removed from the fridge with a non-chilled one from the boxes stacked three deep in the corner. When I opened the fridge it was crammed full of half bottles and we proceeded to work our way through them at a steady pace. Mr John had a friend staying for the weekend – he introduced him to me as a Royal Navy chum from Portsmouth – and having given his chauffeur some time off he summoned a taxi to take us to the Felixstowe Sailing Club. When I asked for a Cobnut, a brown ale drink, Mr John point-blank refused to buy it. I explained I would like to try it and again he said no. When I persisted he raised his voice to state, "It's bloody horrible and I should know – I fucking brew the stuff!" There was no answer to that.

Several drinks later we headed for the Orwell House Hotel in Felixstowe, only to discover the dining room deserted, except for a chap using a vacuum cleaner as part of the regular afternoon clean-up operation.

I would have turned round and headed for the exit, but Mr John instead staggered up to him, grabbed the cleaner and told him, "Let me do that. You pop into the kitchen and drum up some lunch for the three of us, there's a good chap." Roast beef and all the trimmings duly arrived and we later returned to Capel Hall, where we consumed more champagne until after midnight. The pace was pretty hectic and, being short of practice, I have to confess I lagged a fair bit behind but still suffered a massive hangover the next day.

I had been at the club for less than six months when I was invited to attend the annual Professional Footballers' Association awards dinner, which was being held at the Hilton Hotel in London's Park Lane. It was 1975 and Mr John hosted two tables at what was, and still is, one of the highlights of the game's social calendar and part of which, the section when the various awards were presented, was screened live by ITV. I had watched the previous year's event on the box and seen Kevin Beattie collect the Young Player of the Year accolade, and here I was sitting alongside him. *It most certainly is a funny old game*, I recall thinking to myself.

I have a vivid recollection of that night, the first of many as Ipswich basked in their reputation as a fun club and, as far I could ascertain, by far the most generous in terms of picking up what must been a hefty tab. As we took our seats for the function, I was sat directly opposite Mr John and we were asked to be upstanding as the top table guests entered the room from an area behind me. I was absolutely flabbergasted when, after some of football's biggest names passed by immediately to my right, Mr John greeted one of them, who was still not visible to me, with the words, "Hello c**t face!" As the mystery figure stopped, bringing the procession to a stuttering halt, I looked to see who it was and straight away recognised him as none other than Alan Hardaker, the autocratic secretary of the Football League and a man with a public reputation for being a rather crusty, cantankerous character. But on this occasion, albeit briefly, Mr Hardaker's face broke into a huge grin and he revealed a sense of fun, chuckling as he replied, "Hello John, you old bugger. How are you? We must have a drink later on."

That was merely the opening salvo on a night of many incidents, none more amusing than when the official proceedings were over and Mr John asked me to round up the players for a party in his room. Unfortunately, because the players were keen to mingle with other professionals, some of them former colleagues, my efforts to cajole them into attending Mr John's impromptu shindig fell on deaf ears. Clearly impatient, Mr John arrived back in the still crowded function room approximately 20 minutes later, wearing his striped pyjamas and with his ticket stuffed between his lips, muttering, "Am I too late? Is the party over?" There was much hilarity at his appearance and it had the desired effect, prompting the players to follow him back to his room, where he emptied the entire contents of his fridge into the waste paper bin, which we could only hope he had remembered to rinse out earlier. Mixing his extremely potent concoction with the handle of his toothbrush, he handed out paper cups and urged his guests, "Tuck in, boys. I've made us some punch."

As far as I am aware, Mr John conducted a lifelong love affair with alcohol. He was also a heavy smoker and I often chuckled to myself upon hearing or reading a news item about the now implemented Government ban on smoking in public places, including football grounds. How on earth, I wondered, would he react to being told he could not light up anywhere inside Portman Road, especially when it was rare to see him without a cigarette in his hand?

His other addiction was laughter and I remember how television star Jim Davidson was absolutely gobsmacked upon meeting Mr John. The popular comedian was the club's guest at a Saturday afternoon game and was suitably wined and dined, although he had to decline much of the hospitality being dispensed, explaining he had a show to do that evening. I was one of several club officials who attended the performance at what is now the Regent Theatre and Jim opened his act by recounting his experience earlier in the day. He cocked back his head and sort of waddled across the stage to mimic Mr John before telling the audience, "You know why he walks like that, don't you? It's to make sure he doesn't spill a single drop."

It was often the case that Mr John would pop his head round the door of my office and invite me to join him for lunch at the club's own restaurant, the Centre Spot, and more often than not in the company of cronies like Charlie Manning, the larger-than-life proprietor of the extensive amusement park in Felixstowe, which is still going strong under the careful eye of his son, Charlie junior. The two men's lives could hardly have been more different, Mr John born into a privileged place in society and Charlie making his own entrance in the back of a caravan in the east end of London. A strong friendship with Billy Butlin, whom he helped to establish the country's first holiday camp in Skegness, led to Charlie moving to Suffolk and he and Mr John quickly became the best of buddies.

To dine in their company was quite an experience. The food was almost incidental and instead I lapped up the conversation, which often centred on their very different childhood memories. Charlie would recall how his love of football started when he would crawl under the turnstiles at Upton Park, the home of West Ham, while Mr John was introduced to football after his father took up the challenge to bring the professional game to Ipswich in 1936 and was, rightly so, the unanimous choice to become the club's first chairman. Charlie bought a season ticket and never used it, instead sitting at Mr John's personal invitation in the directors' box. He was no freeloader, however, and paid for his many complimentary gin and tonics several times over by purchasing a fistful of Golden Goal draw tickets. Invariably, since his chances of winning a prize were so much greater, he would end up with items like autographed footballs and free tickets, which he would always hand back. His generosity also extended to free admission to all club personnel to his amusement park, where the offices were lined with pictures of him rubbing shoulders with royalty and leading showbiz personalities, thanks to his membership of the Variety Club, an organisation he supported enthusiastically until his death.

They might have been opposites in terms of their background and upbringing, but in many ways Charlie and Mr John were two of a kind, since both were fun-loving characters with king-sized personalities, and marvellous raconteurs each blessed with a razor-sharp sense of humour. There were times when Charlie would suggest travelling to an away game in his Bentley and stopping off for dinner en route for home. He and Mr John would often compete in the generosity stakes, the real winners of which were the waiters and waitresses who benefited from some munificent tipping. Charlie had a passion for Melba toast and was appalled if he was ever told it was not available. On the other hand, a positive response from the restaurant staff would ensure they were handsomely rewarded if they came up with the goods. He would jokingly ask them, "Do you take tips?" before licking the tip of the forefinger on his right hand and reaching into the relevant pocket to pull out a £1, £5 or £10 note, much to the delight of its rather embarrassed, but nevertheless pleasantly surprised, recipient.

Mr Patrick did not see eye to eye with Charlie and often referred to him in a derogatory manner as a 'gippo'. Following John's death, Patrick would regularly dine in the Centre Spot, alone in the opposite corner as far away as possible from Charlie, who was genuinely hurt at such treatment, as he often admitted when I spoke to him about it. Indeed, I don't think my friendship with Charlie did me any favours, although I have no regrets. After Bobby's departure in June 1982 and Mr John's death 15 months later the club seemed unable to recover from such a massive double blow. I was declared redundant in September 1984 and Patrick never even broke the news to me personally. He had departed for a shooting holiday in Scotland and assigned the task to director John Kerr, who was to admit to me years later that he had hated being the messenger. I soon discovered the redundancy was a sham, not least because the club advertised for my successor within a few days, something that at least enabled me to negotiate a proper severance agreement rather than simply walk away, as the club rather naively felt I would. I recall breaking the news of my impending departure to Bobby, who was attending an Ipswich home game in his role as England manager, and how he told me, "This would never have happened if I was still here and Mr John had not passed away."

My days at Portman Road were often punctuated with a visit from Mr John. If he didn't ask me to join him for lunch he would invariably invite me to the boardroom for a drink. "Come and have a glass of port," he would say, making it sound like an order rather than a request. It was my belief that he was lonely and seeking some company, and there were times when the club secretary, David Rose, and Bobby would also be there. We would chew the fat about the issues of the day. On one occasion I recall Mr John popping into my office and it happened to be later in the afternoon on the day the Chancellor of the Exchequer had delivered his eagerly awaited Budget speech. Mr John maintained a stern look on his face as he said, "Have you heard the news? It's preposterous. Do you know what they've done? They've only gone and put up the price of food by 50 pence a bottle!"

It was not everyone who shared Mr John's perception of the good life. I wasn't around at the time, but I love the tale of a chairman of a northern club – I believe he was referred to as Alderman Entwistle – who was paying his first visit to Portman Road. It was a fixture at the start of the 1957/58 season, Mr John having taken over as chairman in May 1957, at the tender age of 29, which meant he was the youngest chairman in the entire Football League. He was no respecter of tradition, bringing an interesting new approach to the role that saw him discard the 'rule' book and do things his way.

The story goes that Mr John was there to greet all visitors, including the immaculately turned out Alderman Entwistle, sporting a charcoal suit, bowler hat and with a watch and chain tucked into his waistcoat pocket. Mr John was dressed far more modestly and upon introducing himself as the Ipswich chairman he was given a perplexed look by his opposite number. Things were no better as Mr John asked, "Would you like a drink? Or perhaps a cigar?" Alderman Entwistle was far from impressed and replied, "Nay, lad. Ne'er a drop of alcohol has ever passed my lips and smoking's for chimneys." That was Mr John's cue to respond, "In which case, sir, we have absolutely nothing in common. I bid you good day." The pair later occupied their respective front row seats, just a couple of feet apart, on either side of the directors' box gangway, without exchanging another word all afternoon.

Not all visitors to Portman Road were able to resist the warmth of Mr John's welcome, the hospitality dispensed by the glass and long into the night. Many an opposition team bus was kept waiting for directors to board and on more than one occasion a visiting manager had to be assisted back to the vehicle much the worse for wear. The inner sanctum was a no-go area for women as the Cobbold brothers held court and invitations to join the throng were much sought after, although some recipients quickly came to regret the experience as they were mercilessly humiliated as the butt of a number of jokes.

Some national newspaper journalists regarded it as a major scoop to be summoned but one regular, Robert (Bob) Oxby of the *Daily Telegraph*, was actually banned by his sports editor from attending matches at Portman Road because he feared for his well-being. There were many times when I dug Bob out of a hole, firstly by keeping him up to date with events on the pitch and then by ensuring he made it to Ipswich station in time to catch the last train to London. Typically, Mr John loved my suggestion that perhaps it would be a good idea if future press passes incorporated a health warning.

Mr John's favourite greeting, even if he was meeting someone for the first time, was to grab the other person's tie and pretend to blow his nose in it. He always got away with it. He detested pretentiousness in any shape or form and when they were served champagne in the Old Trafford boardroom by Louis Edwards they were far from impressed when the Manchester United chairman drew their attention to his personalised labels. "Oh fuck off Louis, that's nothing," Mr John rejoiced in telling him, "we've had fucking millions of bottles with our name on them."

Most other club directors looked forward to their annual trip to Portman Road and there were very few to whom Mr John did not roll out the red carpet. This minority group included Peter Swales, the rather gruff chairman of Manchester City, and I recall how the mischievous brothers plotted for weeks ahead of the Sky Blues' visit. They eventually decided that the highlight of the pre-match meal attended by the directors of both clubs would be Lancashire Hotpot and they chuckled for days ahead of the game. When I caught up with Mr John afterwards I asked how lunch had gone. "Regrettably, rather too well," he replied. "The joke rebounded somewhat because bloody Swales enjoyed it so much that he asked for more!"

Watford's promotion to the First Division in the early 80s was another reason to plan a special meal. They could not wait to welcome the bewigged Elton John in his role as the Hornets' chairman and ordered the Centre Spot chef to prepare hare (hair) soup and to ensure there were fairy cakes for afters. Elton, who apparently appreciated the joke, revealed in a newspaper interview, years later, that he was not, as many people had speculated, the only homosexual football club chairman, adding that he knew of at least one other and identifying Mr John.

The chairman's sexuality was not a topic that was discussed at the club, although I remember him telling me a classic story that, at the very least, suggested he was indeed gay. He was a leading light behind the scenes at the annual East of England International Championships hosted by Felixstowe Lawn Tennis Club and which, over the years, has attracted a number of leading players in the early stages of their careers, among them the former British number one Tim Henman. Hundreds of young players from across the globe descended on the seaside town in search of valuable ranking points and Mr John threw open the doors of his home to several guests, among them a handsome young American player who decided to sample the local night life.

At around 2am Mr John was awoken by a noise at his window and upon investigating he realised that someone was directing small stones at it to attract his attention. He opened the curtains, threw up the window and there, outside the front door, was the young man from the USA in tow with a girl he had met earlier in Felixstowe. "Gee, Mr John, I'm real sorry for coming home late and waking you, but I don't have a key," said the visitor, at which point Mr John said he would come down to open the front door. Upon doing that, the young man ushered his female friend inside before whispering in Mr John's ear, "I hope you don't mind me asking, but you don't happen to have a condom, do you?" When he recounted the story, Mr John delighted in adding, "I didn't mind one bit that he asked. In fact I was actually rather flattered that he thought I would have such a thing as a rubber Johnny about my person!"

Although always polite and courteous when in the company of women, it was clear that Mr John was not interested in the opposite sex. He was never happier than when holding court at the bar, drink in one hand and cigarette in the other, recounting one story after another. The same could not be said of his fellow directors and some were known to occasionally stray on away trips. I remember how Brian Simpson, the club physiotherapist, and I were having an evening drink in a hotel bar near Derby prior to the next day's game at the Baseball Ground when two women who we took to be ladies of the night entered and headed straight to the bar. As they sipped their drinks and left little to the imagination, thanks to the way the neon light rendered their skirts virtually transparent, Brian and I were summoned to reception for the taxi we had ordered a few minutes earlier to transport us to a local night club.

As we left the bar two directors were entering and I mischievously said, "Watch out, a couple of prostitutes over there" and at that their pace immediately quickened. Brian and I thought nothing more of it but when we returned to the hotel around midnight we had to pass the directors' rooms en route to our own and there was no mistaking whose voice we could hear uttering the phrase "Oh that's lovely" over and over again. Upon hearing the story Mr John thought it immensely amusing to occasionally utter the 'catchphrase' within earshot of his fellow director. That same director almost landed me in trouble in Barcelona when I agreed to accompany him to a bar across the road from the city centre hotel where we were based for one of the club's two European clashes with the Catalan giants.

Typically, after we had seen Town lose to exit the competition and made our way back from the Nou Camp, Mr John was first to the hotel bar. We had consumed a few drinks when the other director, a real fun-lover, coaxed me into accompanying him to a bar across the road. He informed me he had been there earlier in the day and that it was well worth a visit. When we went in he headed straight for a particular woman, possibly the manager but clearly an authoritative figure, and as we awaited our drinks he pulled away her elasticated top to reveal two generous breasts and proceeded to stick his head between them, moving his head rapidly from one to the other. Even if the woman did virtually nothing to discourage him – in fact she was giggling with delight – it was deemed a step too far and two burly gents stepped in to remove us pronto. The director was still laughing aloud as we arrived back at the hotel bar to regale his colleagues about the incident.

Mr John's days were rarely complete without a lengthy lunch, most of it liquid, and the club's own restaurant, the Centre Spot, was a particular favourite. This was invariably followed by a boardroom session that would require the port stocks to be replenished. Hard to imagine, perhaps, but I once saw Bobby deliver a dressing down because he feared the chairman would put at risk a major sponsorship deal with the Japanese hi-fi giants, Pioneer.

I had spent many weeks cultivating the relationship between the two parties and a decision was imminent. My presentation to the firm at their then headquarters in Iver, Buckinghamshire, close to Pinewood Studios, famous for the James Bond movies and many others, had gone well, despite an initial hiccup that stopped me in my tracks. I was in full flow when, with little warning, I was asked to stop and the firm's main man, none other than the world president, who was over from Japan and would have the final say on whether or not the deal would go ahead, left the room with one of his sidekicks. It was a full five minutes before he returned. I noticed he was clutching a copy of what I immediately recognised as an Automobile Association handbook and as he took his seat he waved it in my direction, smiled and said, "Sorry, I just wanted to know where Ipswich is. Now please carry on."

The presentation came many weeks after I had first approached Pioneer about a sponsorship deal and I must admit that at that precise moment I wondered if there was any point in continuing. I was certainly deflated, however I persevered and in the end felt satisfied with the way things had gone. To my huge relief, the Pioneer hierarchy were also keen to continue negotiations and in the end it all came down to a crucial meeting to take place in the boardroom at Portman Road, followed by dinner in the Centre Spot, where staff were under strict instructions to put on a special show.

The entire board of directors were to be present and because the scheduled meeting happened to coincide with the FA Cup final replay between Tottenham Hotspur and Manchester City a television was strategically placed in the restaurant to enable us to keep up to date with events from Wembley. There was more than passing interest from the Ipswich end since we felt we had lost rather harshly to City in extra-time in the semi-final at Villa Park and some weeks later there was still a feeling that we should have been one of the final participants.

Battle plans were drawn up well in advance and when Bobby joined Mr John and I in the boardroom at around 5pm he was quick to tell the chairman, "I don't want you messing up this deal. Don't have too much to drink and spoil it, will you? There's a lot of money riding on this, don't forget." I feared Mr John might not take kindly to the manager's warning and explode, but instead he just smiled that mischievous smile and told Bobby, "Don't you worry about a thing."

I had been briefed by Pioneer's sales manager, Alan Sexton, as to which members of their board would be in attendance at the meeting and he informed me that he would lead them into the boardroom and, since his directors were meeting mine for the very first time, he would make the introductions.

All the Ipswich personnel arrived in good time and it would not be an exaggeration to say the mood was tentative. When the Pioneer deputation arrived, Alan duly led them into the boardroom, at which point Mr John, upon spotting he was carrying a briefcase, asked, "What have you got in there, Alan? The Japanese ambassador?" The temptation to laugh was irresistible but fortunately the giggles were stifled before a series of diminutive guests followed on. Bobby and I looked at each other as if to say, 'I think we got away with that one,' but it was clear Mr John had been drinking non-stop since lunchtime and had taken absolutely no notice of Bobby's well-intended pep talk.

As the evening progressed the two sides were gelling as I had hoped they would but, typically, it was Mr John who stole the show as he stood to make a brief speech. "I am very sorry, everyone, but I must leave now," he announced. "I have the Duke of Kent staying with me and he will think it rather rude of me if I leave it any later before returning home." Mr Patrick also apologised and departed with his brother, although any concern I might have felt that their early withdrawal would put a dampener on the deal was quickly dispelled.

They had only been gone a second or two before Pioneer's managing director piped up. "Did he say Duke of Kent? He knows Duke of Kent? Duke of Kent staying with him?" At this point Bobby Robson had the undivided attention of the Pioneer delegation as he escorted them on a fleeting and fascinating journey through the Cobbold family tree. He explained that Mr John and Mr Patrick had strong royal family links, that their mother, Lady Blanche, was the daughter of the 9th Duke of Devonshire and that their uncle was Harold Macmillan, the former Prime Minister, who married Lady Blanche's sister, Lady Dorothy.

It was as if his words cast a magical spell over the Pioneer people and it was clear they were very impressed. I have absolutely no doubt that Bobby's crash course on the Cobbold dynasty helped to persuade them to proceed with a three-year sponsorship that, when it was announced, was the biggest in British football. At the press conference to announce the £600,000 deal, on the eve of the 1981/82 season, which was attended by Fleet Street's finest, Mr John announced, "People have asked what we are going to do with the money. We intend to spend some on wine, women and song, and we shall probably squander the rest."

Mr John decided to resign as chairman of Ipswich Town in the summer of 1976, after 19 years in the role, and hand over to his brother. It was a source of much joy and hilarity to the pair that Ipswich won the FA Cup for the first time in their history in May 1978, to signal a triumphant end to only Mr Patrick's second season as chairman. I remember a magazine interview with Mr Patrick and Mr John, at which I was also present, and the young journalist, Trevor Haylett, now one of the country's most distinguished football correspondents, was clearly taken aback by their rather frivolous attitude. Turning to Mr John he said, "You used to be chairman, so what is your present position?" Before he had a chance to answer, Mr Patrick stated, "Fucking dodgy now that I'm in charge." It was a tough baptism for Trevor and one on which I am certain he has often reflected with great amusement.

Mr John tended to shun the media spotlight but there were occasions when there was no hiding place and he had no alternative. I remember a well known national newspaper correspondent pinning him down for long enough to garnish material for a feature and it proved to be a real battle of wits. He was asked how many board meetings the club held in a year and he replied, "Two or three." The journalist persisted by asking how many would be held if the team was performing badly and was stunned when Mr John told him, "We wouldn't have any at all." Mr John said each win was celebrated by cracking open a bottle of champagne and when he was asked how he consoled himself in defeat he said, "I open two bottles, of course."

The family home at Glemham Hall was opened to the public each year and the brothers would occasionally be there on a Sunday afternoon, when the grounds were swarming with people. They were relaxing one day, snoozing on the lawn behind broadsheet newspapers, when they heard a rare commotion. They would much rather have been able to maintain their anonymity than intervene but eventually felt they had no alternative. A woman customer was complaining to a member of staff about the condition of a fruit scone she had purchased along with a pot of tea. Mr John tried to mediate and asked the disgruntled woman if there was anything he could do to help. "Look at my scone," said the woman angrily, "it's got dust on it." Mr John studied it carefully before replying, "No, madam. That's not dust, it's mouse shit!"

One of Mr John's prized possessions was a letter that he had received from a season ticket holder in the 60s and which he was still carrying in a wallet right up to the time of his death more than 20 years later. The supporter was concerned that the manager at the time, Jackie Milburn, who succeeded League Championship-winning boss Alf Ramsey, was signing too many Scottish players. Jackie had gone to Raith Rovers and signed a goalkeeper, Jim Thorburn, only for him to concede goals at an alarming rate – a whopping 36 in his nine league appearances during the 1963/64 season – as the team headed towards relegation from the First Division just two years after having won the title.

Thorburn was not solely responsible for this depressing state of affairs – the truth of the matter was that Ramsey left Milburn a team past its sell-by date – but he made the ideal scapegoat in the eyes of the letter writer, who happened to have been temporarily resident in Scotland prior to the goalkeeper's transfer south of the border. Mr John showed me the letter, in which the none-too-amused fan observed, 'Thorburn has had more balls through his hands than the Duchess of Argyll.' Once I had read it and smiled, Mr John whooped with laughter and carefully folded it before returning it to his wallet, a routine he had probably performed hundreds of times since it had come into his possession.

Mr John and Bobby had a healthy respect for one another and enjoyed a wonderful working relationship, but occasionally Bobby would feel that Mr John overstepped the mark. One such occasion was when Ipswich arranged a friendly game against Celtic at Parkhead in November 1976 and we were en route for the airport to fly to Scotland. Mr John was in a particularly playful mood and it was his idea to instigate a competition to find the best limerick, including the name of a football club, and several players, among them Northern Ireland international Allan Hunter, a born comedian, were quick to respond. Bobby was sat in his usual seat at the front and the commotion ensued immediately behind him, with a succession of limericks, together with bursts of laughter, gradually getting to him. Eventually his patience cracked and he turned round to deliver a brief rant. Mr John said nothing while Bobby spoke but once he had finished calmly said, "Right, carry on chaps!"

I know of only one occasion when Mr John felt it necessary to intervene in an effort to defuse a potentially explosive situation. In September 1980 I felt extremely sorry for the manager when he held his usual post-match press briefing. We had beaten Coventry 2-0 through two second-half goals by John Wark, but the Ipswich fans were strangely subdued during what was our sixth success in an unbeaten start to the season. Ipswich led the league but undoubtedly there were times when the supporters frustrated Bobby and this was one of them. He always said that Ipswich was a club where the team had to get the fans going, whereas at other clubs the opposite was the case and the vocal contribution from the terraces often inspired the players to perform. "They are Zombies here," he said in a rather unfortunate turn of phrase, and of course the inevitable happened. The word was used in the headline of virtually every newspaper report the next day and again on the Monday. Some supporters objected and the club, together with the local newspapers, were bombarded with complaints. "You must apologise," said Mr John. But Bobby was reluctant and argued against such a move. "I insist," said Mr John, and the apology was duly issued. As it turned out, some fans had badges made that proclaimed, 'I'm an Ipswich Zombie' and their light-hearted response tended to prevail.

Mr John may have given the impression that he did not preside over club affairs as intently as he maybe should have done, but there was absolutely no negligence on his part. He had no office, not even a desk, at

Portman Road and preferred to leave the running of the club to Bobby, who was more like the managing director than merely manager, and other officials. He did not interfere but there were times when he would not hesitate to pull rank and one such occasion occurred during an end-of-season 'jolly'. They were usually to exotic locations like Barbados and Martinique, and I remember how the end of the season would be in sight and the directors would regularly enquire of the manager, "Where are we going this year, Bobby? Any news yet?"

I was not present but received an eye-witness account from Mr John of what took place. He and other directors were enjoying a drink on a hotel terrace with Bobby when there was a message over the hotel loudspeaker, "Would Mr Bobby Robson please come to reception to take a telephone call." No sooner had Bobby departed than a director grabbed his attaché case and started to not only remove the contents but rifle through them. Mr John was aghast at his colleague's behaviour and ordered him, "Put that back at once or I shall demand your resignation right here and now." Needless to say the red-faced board member took the chairman's advice and remained a director for many more years. And no, I shall not be revealing his identity.

I was the unwitting victim of Mr John's wicked sense of humour on numerous occasions, but I like to think I gave as good as I got without causing offence. I was firmly in the firing line on one famous occasion, however, and the joke was shared by almost 17,000 people, namely those present at Portman Road for a first-team game against Leicester City on 17 December 1977. A few weeks earlier we had played in Las Palmas, winning through to the third round of the UEFA Cup, and it was an achievement worth celebrating. Having enjoyed a few drinks in the hotel bar, and still feeling rather fragile by the time we took our seats on the plane for the next day's homeward journey, I quickly lapsed into a lengthy sleep. What I didn't know was that Mr John had asked a photographer who accompanied us to take a picture of me, with my mouth gaping open, and to pass it on to our match programme printers with specific instructions for it to appear in a later issue, suitably captioned – Dreaming of a White Christmas? – so as to cause maximum embarrassment to yours truly.

I also recall the one and only occasion when Mr John accompanied me in my car to an away fixture against Nottingham Forest in November 1980. Also present were local newspaper correspondents Dave Allard and Elvin King, with the latter reporting on his very first Ipswich game. The City Ground was neither a very happy hunting ground for Bobby's team, nor many others, during an era in which Brian Clough not only led his team to the domestic title but also back-to-back European Cup successes, but on this particular occasion Town triumphed and no one was more delighted than Mr John.

It was clear to see he had consumed a fair amount of booze before slipping into the passenger seat of my car for the homeward journey, but after we had travelled just a few hundred yards from the car park he ordered me to pull over. I feared he might be feeling unwell but once the car was stationary he wound down the window and shouted towards a group of Forest fans standing nearby. He summoned the group of about six towards the car and as they approached he whispered, "Get ready, Mel." Once they were within a couple of feet he barked out the words, "We've stuffed Clough" and I took that as my signal to accelerate away as fast as my club issue Ford Cortina would allow, with Mr John in hoots of laughter.

The George Hotel at Stamford, not far off the A1, was a favourite venue at which to stop en route for Ipswich after away games and Mr John directed me to do just that. The hotel's food was renowned but, in keeping with someone who would clearly rather drink than eat, he picked at what he had ordered and by the time a waiter removed the plate very little had been consumed. When we adjourned to the lounge for coffee Mr John took great delight in dipping his teaspoon in the cream and flicking it in my general direction, much to the amusement of our travelling companions. Several 'hits' later my suit bore a number of stains but even when we returned to the car to complete the remainder of our journey the fun was far from over. Having deposited Dave and Elvin to their office car park in Ipswich, and with Mr John fast asleep, I had no alternative but to drive to Capel Hall and deliver him home, but not before reaching into his pocket to acquire the key and then carrying him upstairs to his bedroom and despatching him on top of his bed. Mr John was so inebriated that he slept through the entire episode.

My favourite Mr John story? I have narrowed it down to two, which was far from easy, starting with the South East Counties League annual dinner held at the Royal Lancaster Hotel in London and at which Mr John was required to deliver his inaugural speech as president. In those days the South East Counties League was a breeding ground for the next generation of stars, real-life apprentices learning their trade, washing floors, scrubbing toilets and polishing boots during the week but doing what they did best on a Saturday morning. Ipswich won the title regularly from the big London clubs and I remember that when Alan Brazil collected the league's Player of the Year award the list of previous winners included the likes of all-time greats Jimmy Greaves and Bobby Moore.

In other words, it was a prestigious accolade and the dinner reflected the league's standing, attended as it was by most, if not all, the managers of the member clubs to make for an impressive top table. The clubs, in turn, booked tables and I was among the Ipswich contingent, alongside directors and officials, eager to see how Mr John, who had been noticeably edgy for a few days beforehand about having to deliver the presidential address, coped.

Come the big moment, he was introduced and there was an uncomfortable delay as he tried to get to his feet. Clearly under the influence, he finally managed it but before he had a chance to utter even a single word he slid back under the table, completely disappearing from view, and subsequently failed to resurface. No one knew how to react. Some of those present may have feared he had been taken ill, while others might have thought it was all part of the act, given his reputation as a prankster. But on our table we knew the truth. He was out cold as Bobby Robson and, if my memory serves me right, Southampton manager Lawrie McMenemy gathered him up.

At this point the audience got to their feet and bade him farewell with thunderous applause, none of which he heard. Bobby and Lawrie were like a couple of undertakers with a rigid corpse and when they got to the front door of the hotel they were urged to put him in the back of a Rolls Royce that belonged to the Tottenham Hotspur chairman, Sydney Wale, whose chauffeur was asked to take Mr John and Bobby to Liverpool Street station. At Ipswich they were met by Mr John's chauffeur, who did what he had done on countless occasions. He took him home and put him to bed, and when he called round the next morning Mr John could remember nothing of what had occurred the previous night, although when given a blow-by-blow account he rather predictably thought it highly amusing and laughed aloud.

It would take a special tale to top that one and my number one recollection of Mr John is of the speech he delivered at the party to celebrate Ipswich Town's victory in the FA Youth Cup in 1975, the second time in three seasons that the top trophy in youth football had been landed. Typical of Ipswich, and certainly helped by the fact that the team had established a healthy two-goal first leg lead over West Ham in the game at Upton Park, the chairman decided the occasion was worthy of a celebration get-together and invitations were sent to every parent of the members of the youth squad.

They came from far and wide, including Scotland and Northern Ireland, to see their boys triumph in front of more than 16,000 fans at Portman Road and afterwards Mr John presided over an excellent dinner at the Copdock Hotel. As liqueurs were being sipped, Mr John rose to deliver a brief victory speech along the following lines, "A big thank you to the boys and everyone else who has contributed to the club's success. And a big welcome to all you parents – thank you very much indeed for the significant part you have played. Now, without further ado, I suggest you adjourn for the evening. Get yourselves upstairs, have a jolly good fuck and make us a brand new youth team for about 18 years from now." Needless to say, it brought the house down, although a number of parents encountering Mr John for the very first time were simply lost for words.

Mr John: In His Own Words

SOME TIME AGO I told an author friend of mine that I was thinking of writing a book. I asked how I should begin. His answer was that I should command my readers' attention as quickly as possible, preferably on the opening page. So here we go. "Fuck," said the Duchess, waving her wooden leg.

Okay, perhaps not, but several years ago one or two people suggested that I should put down on paper a few of the more amusing, possibly boring and occasionally extraordinary, things that have happened during my lifetime. The second person died a few years ago in a home for the mentally unstable.

I have tried very hard not to offend anyone and I have also tried very hard to use what could be called BBC language or, in these modern days, various words which 20 years ago would have been offensive. In fact, I have only used them when they have been part of various anecdotes. I have also tried to use as few names as possible, being very frightened of the laws of libel and I am absolutely certain that should anybody recognise themselves it will be their own fault, rather than mine, if they do.

This book – if anybody reads it – is mainly devoted to Ipswich Town Football Club and my grateful thanks go to all the people connected with the club for the amusement and assistance they have given not only me but also the club's various managers during my time as director and chairman.

I am also very grateful to people I have met all over the world in various bars, nightclubs, pubs, in the street and even in police stations, who have made remarks that have certainly appealed to my admittedly rather warped sense of humour.

I am especially grateful to Mel Henderson, who is the public relations officer of Ipswich Town and a journalist who is attempting to turn my tapes into readable English. Being a Scotsman, I imagine he will have found that extremely difficult.

Potty Training

I WAS BORN on 30 June 1927. My father was not only a very keen shot, but certainly one of the best shots in the country, and judging by the nine-month interval it would appear that I was conceived at the end of the grouse shooting and the start of the partridge shooting. He used to kill most of the flying birds with one barrel, but I am not quite sure how many barrels I took. Not only was 1927 a very good year for John Cavendish* Cobbold, it was also an excellent year for vintage port and apparently, when I was half an hour old, I was given a pen-filler of brandy and we haven't really looked back since.

*Mr John earned the middle name Cavendish because of a family tradition that the first-born son would take his mother's maiden name as his middle one.

Unlike that marvellous character, Gerard Hoffnung*, who stated that he was two when he was born and then died far too early at the age of just 34, I was born when I was aged nought. Apparently my mother took one look at me and said I looked like a monkey, while my father, who was also a very keen fisherman, allegedly asked, or at least wondered, if I shouldn't be put back.

I thought I would start with my early life and more or less go through it until the present day because as I grew up in age (possibly not mentally) more and more things seemed to happen. This has led to my final thoughts – well, I hope not final, because at this moment in time I am still very much alive – as far as this book is concerned. I very much doubt if there will ever be another one.

My first recollection is of being put on a potty behind the sofa in the nursery at Glemham Hall**, where I used to live, and my grandfather or

---

*Berlin-born Gerard Hoffnung was an artist and musician best known for his humorous works, among them a series of books of cartoons in which his 'victims' were conductors and orchestral instrumentalists. He was born in March 1925, the only child of a well-to-do Jewish couple, and died of a cerebral haemorrhage in September 1959, just 20 years after the family moved to London. Like Mr John, he was known for his eccentricity and as a public speaker was much in demand by the Oxford and Cambridge Unions.

**According to its official website, Glemham Hall is an elegant, red brick Elizabethan mansion, which originally belonged to the Glemham family, who took their name from the adjacent villages of Great Glemham and Little Glemham. In 1923 it was purchased by the Cobbold family and became the home of Mr John's father, Captain John (known as Ivan) Murray Cobbold and his wife Lady Blanche, who had a staff of more than 20 servants. When Lady Blanche died in 1987, the estate passed to her son, Patrick, and when he passed away in 1994 it was inherited by his nephew, Major Philip Hope-Cobbold, formerly Hope-Johnstone, who lives there with his wife, Raewyn, originally from New Zealand. Major Hope-Cobbold was born in the Hall in 1943, attended the Royal Military Academy Sandhurst and served with the 13th/18th Royal Hussars (Queen Mary's Own) until 1992. Today he is a patron of Ipswich Town Football Club and the Hall has become a popular venue for weddings and many corporate events.

godfather coming in and asking we what I was doing. I have to say that even in those early days when I was aged about three I thought it was a completely unnecessary question. I was always devoted to my nanny*, who in those days virtually looked after all the children, and I remember well that whenever she had an evening off to go down to the village whist drive I used to howl and scream, bellow and blub. As regards blubbing, I still do at anything like a royal funeral, the Trooping of the Colour, winning the FA Cup or something dramatic happening. I admit I burst into tears and enjoy every second of it.

In spite of the fact that it could be said I was born with a silver spoon in my mouth, I appeared to have either the back of a Mason Pearson hairbrush or a ruler hitting my backside far more than I ever had any type of spoon in my mouth, even when consuming Cow & Gate. In those days the practice of being seen and not heard was definitely the mode. There was no such thing as playschool or kindergarten; we were put under the control of a governess and in my family's case she was a very formidable lady who frightened the living daylights out of us.

The morning was entirely restricted to lessons in reading, writing and arithmetic – quite rightly in my view – while in the afternoon we were made to lie on our backs on the floor on dust sheets. This was meant to keep our backs straight and what else it kept straight I have never been quite sure. After this dramatic experience of lying on the floor in the school room we were then taken, both girls and boys, upstairs, changed into skirts and taken back downstairs to see the grown-ups for tea. Why I was put into a skirt I

---

*Mr John's nanny was Alice Moore, although she was called Nanny Moore or by her nickname of Blossom. She remained at Glemham Hall long after her retirement and died there when she was in her 80s.

will never know because I much preferred what other people had, a sailor's outfit, or even a kilt. As everybody knows, a kilt is a type of Scottish skirt and I even have a bit of Scottish blood in me.

Another ghastly episode that we had to go through in the fairly early hours of the morning was to ride. Having been absolutely terrified – always have been and still am – of horses and ponies, because I consider them to be dangerous at both ends as well as bloody uncomfortable in the middle, this wasn't my scene at all. I was fully aware that the horse or pony was far bigger and stronger than I was and was quite capable of taking complete control, as it frequently did. There was one horse I was made to ride called Bows, a name I shall never forget, and whenever he saw a puddle he used to decide to roll in it, which made it very difficult for the rider on top who had to show the utmost agility.

When I was about seven years old I was made to enter my pony, with me on top, into one of the local horse shows and to everybody's amazement, including my own, I won the first prize, which was obviously entirely due to the efforts of the pony. The following year I was again made to enter the same competition and on this occasion I only came second. The lady who was judging was one of those very *femme formidable* types, dressed in a top hat with veil and riding side saddle. My memory is vague but I am told that because I hadn't won I called her a "bloody old bitch" and the remark was overheard by the groom, who took me to the back of the show ring and beat me soundly with a hunting crop. This was then reported to my father, of whom I was extremely fond, and he also beat me. My father asked where I had learned such language and I told him, "From you daddy," at which point he beat me again. I began to wonder if in those days justice was really done and if I would vote for corporal punishment now.

After all this nothing much happened in my life until I was sent to a private school, Wellesley House* in Broadstairs, Kent. People say that the happiest days of one's life are spent at school but I am afraid I cannot agree. I found it a thoroughly miserable experience to be sent so far away from home. I recall being at Victoria Station, armed with my suitcase and my tuck box, and thinking how I was being sent away from home for the first time. I think my mother was equally upset because, after our fond farewells and the train had left, she discovered she was still sitting on top of my tuck box.

Having arrived at our destination the entire school, about 70 of us, were taken into the dining room and made to sing hymns. They were the most beautiful tunes and to this day, whenever I hear them, I always blub. We were also made to write a letter home saying that we had arrived safely and had tea. To be honest, tea was the best part about it. I always ended up my letter by pleading: 'Please come down immediately and take me home, otherwise I will walk it.' Eventually I was put into a dormitory with about 15 to 20 other boys and as soon as we had cried ourselves to sleep we were woken up by someone having a pee into a tin pot, one of which was neatly placed under every bed. It can't have been hygienic and cannot have done the springs on the bed a great deal of good.

*According to its official website, the entry book at Wellesley goes back to 1866 when the school was called Conyngham House and was sited in Ramsgate. The present building was constructed in its earliest form in 1898. Just before the First World War the school was sold to the then Headmaster, Shirley Russell. Two of the partners, Herbert Day and Leonard Moon, the international cricketer and footballer, were killed in the war. Mr John is not listed in the section headed Alumni but those who are include cricketer Chris Cowdrey, captain of Kent and England, photographer Lord (Patrick) Litchfield, pop star Mike d'Abo, best known as lead singer with Manfred Mann, former newsreader Reginald Bosanquet, HRH The Duke of Gloucester, Sir Peter de la Billiere, who was Commander-in-Chief of the British forces in the 1990 Gulf War and Henry Bellingham, the Conservative MP for North West Norfolk. Girls were not admitted until 1977.

The main lessons we were taught were reading, writing, algebra, geometry, Latin and Greek. Reading and writing I could cope with, because I already knew how to do it, but the languages were completely beyond me and, what's more, still are. If ever I go to Italy or Greece these days and try speaking in Latin or Greek, I might as well be speaking Hindustani. They also tried to teach us sports, which as far as I was concerned was a complete failure. They tried to teach me to swim and I still can't, they tried to teach me to play cricket and I still can't, and when they tried to teach me to play rugger I only played it once and burst into tears in the middle of the scrum, which was a very damp experience for the others. I was, however, a little bit better at soccer and got into the fifth XI. I considered that to be a great achievement, considering there was also a sixth XI.

Then the Second World War intervened and we were all, the entire school, evacuated* up to Scotland where my father had three or four hunting lodges that he very kindly gave to the school. Those days were the best of my school life. The entire school went up to Rannoch Station, near Pitlochry in Perthshire, and we travelled by rail in third class sleepers that consisted of four bunks, two up and two down. The masters and the matron were in first class sleepers, as was my father who accompanied us. He had very kindly placed a one pound bar of milk chocolate on every boy's bunk and, as I heard later, he had also purchased several large

---

*The Wellesley House official website confirms: 'Although Shirley Russell was still Headmaster in 1939 it was John Boyce and his assistant Billy Williamson who saw the school through the Second World War, evacuating to three hunting lodges at Rannoch. During the war the Army took over the school building at Broadstairs and in 1946 the evacuees returned.'

hampers full of food and drink from Fortnum and Mason* in London's Piccadilly, which was eagerly consumed by the masters and the lady staff. After that, of course, the inevitable happened. We boys, in the shortest possible time, gobbled up our chocolate. We were violently sick and in urgent need of the matron. Unfortunately, however, she was absolutely plastered by the time the train reached Grantham, so we had no alternative but to fend for ourselves. We eventually ended up at Rannoch Station, much to the amazement of the locals, and were carted off by bus to the various lodges where we were to be living. Like I said, they were the best days of my life at school. Being the son of the Laird I was called Little Laird and managed to do the minimum amount of work without getting into too much trouble.

During my time in Scotland I was allowed out and managed to shoot my first stag. It must have been the unluckiest stag in the world because once we had dragged it back to the larder, had it skinned and its head removed – the head was then boiled so that I could get hold of the antlers as a souvenir – it was discovered that the only bullet I had fired had gone down its left lughole. There was another occasion at Rannoch when I was taken out to shoot my first grouse, on 12 August, the traditional start of the grouse shooting season. I must have fired off about 50 cartridges at these damned little black things and not even a tail feather came out, absolutely nothing until we were walking back down the path in the twilight and a

---

*Established in 1707 at 181 Piccadilly, London, by William Fortnum and Hugh Mason, the Fortnum and Mason department store is one of the most famous in the world. It is the shop most closely associated with the royal family and has held many royal warrants for more than 150 years. It is renowned for its luxury picnic hampers, which the store first distributed to Victorian High Society for events such as Henley Regatta and Ascot Races. At today's prices they can cost as much as £25,000 depending on their contents.

snipe got up and wriggled away at great speed. I fired off one cartridge and the thing dropped stone dead, at which point the old keeper turned round to me and said, "Och, that'll teach the old bugger to fly crooked."

Several years ago at Capel Hall*, my home in Suffolk, I gave a party for the village school children and we hired a conjuror. After he had performed various tricks he asked if he could have a volunteer from the audience. No little boy or girl got up so I gave Mr Bixby, our head keeper, a great kick and said, "Go on, off you go and start the ball rolling." He climbed onto the stage and the conjuror greeted him with a handshake before asking, "What would you say, Mr Bixby, if I produced a live rabbit out of your pocket?"

Mr Bixby replied, "I'd say that would be a bloody miracle because I've got my ferret in there."

---

*Capel Hall stands on a peninsula between the Orwell and Deben estuaries. It features 28 bedrooms, stands in 2,000 acres and its construction started in 1464. Its first owner was Sir William Amberville and it was bought by Thomas Cobbold in 1735. Upon his death in 1983, Mr John left it to his nephew, Charles Hope-Johnstone, who died of AIDS in 1994. In 2001 it was bought by a multi-millionaire local businessman, Glyn Davies.

Off To Eton

AFTER, OR IT might have been during, all the frolics I had up at Rannoch, I had to pass my common entrance examination to go to Eton*. This I managed to do, but only just. I obtained a middle fourth grading, which indicated slightly below average, but at least I made it to Eton, a remarkable place, although I can't really say I enjoyed it. One of the most wonderful things about Eton is not only the discipline, but also the self-discipline, the amount of free time one is given, the variety of sport in which one is allowed to partake and the extraordinary number of people of every type one meets there. It is an amazing place for making friends and also, possibly, enemies. Thankfully it is the friendships that tend to last for a very long time.

*Mr John and his brother, Patrick, both attended Eton College, as their father had done. Indeed, the Cobbold connection with Eton dates back to the early 19th century. Mr John's nephews, Ivan and David Paul, were also pupils at Eton, as was David Sheepshanks, who went on to become chairman of Ipswich Town between 1995 and 2009.

Speaking in hindsight, it is quite extraordinary what used to happen to me. As I have already stated, at one moment I was sent away from Kent to the north of Scotland to avoid the bombs, yet just over a year later I was sent to Eton, which was right on the direct path for the German aeroplanes that had every intention of bombing Windsor Castle. I suppose that's how things go. Luckily, although two bombs did land on Eton during my time there, nobody was hurt and very little damage was done.

It was on 18 June 1944, while I was attending Eton, that the biggest disaster, so far, in my life occurred. We had been to evening chapel on a Sunday and as we were coming out there was a rumour going round that the Guards Chapel* had been hit by a flying bomb. I knew that my father occasionally went there and in the evening my housemaster came into my room and said, "Johnny, I have some bad news for you." I must have

---

*The Royal Military Chapel, better known as the Guards Chapel, stands in Birdcage Walk and is the religious home of the Royal Guardsmen based at Wellington Barracks. It is close to Buckingham Palace and on 30 April 1909 Mr John's parents, Captain John (Ivan) Murray Cobbold and Lady Blanche Katherine Cavendish, were married there. It was bombed during the Blitz and the Luftwaffe struck again in 1944. Apart from claiming the lives of 121 military and civilians, a further 141 were seriously injured. An eye-witness account from a doctor who attended said it was initially feared that everyone had been killed. He also said how lifelike the dead Guards' Bandsmen looked. They were playing in the gallery at the side of the Chapel, where the blast had probably killed them by bursting their lungs, but they were in their original positions, holding their instruments, in natural colour as if made of wax. It took two days to dig out the dead and only the Bishop of Maidstone, who was conducting the service, was totally unhurt as he was sheltered by a portico that survived and forms part of the rebuilt structure. Captain Cobbold had invited his friend Stanley Rous to attend the service but he was unable to do so. Knighted for his services to football by King George VI in 1949, Sir Stanley officiated at the FA Cup final of 1934. He then became secretary of the Football Association until 1962 and was president of FIFA, the game's ruling body, through to 1974. Suffolk-born, in Mutford in 1895, he died in Guildford in 1986 at the age of 91.

had a premonition because I turned round to him and said, "I know, sir, my father has been killed." The housemaster replied, "You are quite right."

For some unknown reason, despite the fact that I was absolutely devoted to my father and really adored him, I did not burst into tears, nor did I break down. I can't think why. It may be possible – I was approaching my 17th birthday at the time – that one suddenly realises, as if being given a great slap, that one suddenly has an awful lot of responsibility. The chapel had been packed for the Waterloo Day service and the second lesson was being read by Lord Edward Hay who, along with 121 others, including my father, was killed as the German V-1 flying bomb struck the roof and caused virtually the whole building to fall.

Both my sisters, who were older than me, were in the Auxiliary Territorial Service (ATS)*. I was the oldest son and heir, and my first thoughts were for my poor mother and the awful responsibilities that were going to overtake her in the future. That may be the reason why I felt moderately cool, calm and collected about the whole thing. My mother showed quite incredible courage and determination. She was obviously terribly upset but she also had the frightful problem that, in spite of the fact that my father was practically killed in action, there were still enormous death duties to pay.

---

*Like their male soldier counterparts, the women wore a khaki uniform. ATS members worked as drivers and cleaners, in mess halls – many had to peel potatoes – and on anti-aircraft guns. By July 1942, the ATS had 217,000 women in it and as the war dragged on they became welders, carpenters, electricians etc. Mr John's sister, Jean, was chauffeuse to Sir Drummond Inglis, one of Field Marshall Montgomery's aides, and she also took part in the D-Day landings, served in Arnhem and was one of the first ATS personnel to arrive in Berlin at the end of the war.

She had to battle with accountants, solicitors and auditors on how to raise the money to pay the death duties. Certain things had to be sold – quite a bit of our estate at Rannoch had to go – and various other places that we had on long leases also went. My mother was obviously determined that our home and the land around it, at Glemham in Suffolk, and my present home near Trimley, should remain in the family. She was also determined that the brewery, which in those days was just Cobbold & Co.*, should remain so. She had battle after battle and all the family will be eternally grateful to her because, being a very forcible lady typical of the Cavendish family, she won.

Eventually I left Eton and was called into the army, although I shall never forget the amusing incident that occurred on my very last day. It was too late to be sacked because the headmaster had already presented us with our leaving books. If anybody knows the layout of Eton, there was a very narrow lane called Keats Lane and on each side of it there were two houses, each of which was used to accommodate pupils. One evening,

---

*It was in 1723 that the first Cobbold brewery was founded in Harwich by Thomas Cobbold, a maltster by profession. The business grew to the extent that between the two world wars it operated 270 licenced premises, although after the death of Captain Ivan Cobbold in 1944 the number dropped to 110. In 1957 the Tollemache and Cobbold breweries merged to become Tolly Cobbold. Mr John was briefly chairman and then became production director until 1977, when the business was sold to the shipping company Ellerman Lines for £5.7 million. Six years later, when twin brothers David and Frederick Barclay bought the business, it was worth almost £50 million. In 1989 Tolly Cobbold was sold again, this time to Brent Walker's Grand Metropolitan Group, run by George Walker, brother of ex-heavyweight boxer Billy 'Golden Boy' Walker. It was suggested at the time that the firm was sold for little more than £2 million. More than 100 of the pubs were sold and in 1990 the business was the subject of a business buy-out. In June 2001 the company was taken over by T D Ridley & Sons Limited of Hartford End, near Chelmsford, which became part of the Greene King empire in 2005.

indeed our very last there, we went round all the houses collecting as many china chamber pots as possible, together with a generous length of rope. We threaded the rope through the handles of the pots then pulled it up to one side of Keats Lane and through a window, which we then locked. Our next move was to cut off the end of the rope with a razor blade. We then did exactly the same in the house on the other side of the lane, which took a huge effort by all of us as the rope was extremely heavy. Think about it – how are you going to get that lot down without causing a commotion?

The following morning we all got up fairly early and about half a dozen of us, all wearing our Old Etonian ties as we knew we were safe, sat on a wall to see how the problem would be solved. Eventually, along came the corporation. They tried going up a ladder, but clearly the weight was too much for them. It obviously wasn't worth bringing in a crane, so what would they do? Eventually, having given the matter a great deal of thought, they had no alternative but to go into one of the houses and smash open the window. The inevitable happened and the whole lot came crashing down and you have never seen so many broken china pots in all your life.

What do I really remember about being at Eton? The first thing is the number of air raid sirens that seemed to go off. They appeared to go off every hour or so and to begin with we all had to troop down to the air raid shelters. Eventually it was decided that this was a waste of time and not particularly good for our education so apparently it was arranged that there was a bell connected to Windsor Castle, which also went off at Eton, and all we were required to do was to get under our desks, although I have no idea what protection they would have offered. If it was during darkness we had to turn out the lights as well.

I will always remember there was a master who tried to teach us French, whose name was Monsieur Lezaire. He was a pompous little

Frenchman and one day the air raid siren went, whereupon we disappeared under our desks and the lights went out. After half an hour the all-clear was given, the lights were turned on again and Monsieur Lezaire was minus his trousers, which were later found out in the street having been thrown from the classroom window. To this day I don't know who did it. I know it wasn't me, although I have to confess that I rather wish it had been.

As it was, during the war quite a lot of younger masters had gone off to fight for their country so some of the older ones who had retired were recalled to try to teach us mob. There was one marvellous character called Gerry Churchill, who I believe was a relative of the great Sir Winston Churchill. Poor Gerry Churchill had the most appalling lisp, which made it much too easy for us boys to mimic him. Whenever we were in his class we used to start sucking our pencils and he would invariably demand, "Stop fucking your pencils." It happened time after time – every one a coconut!

Amongst all the other games played at Eton, there were two in particular that are not played anywhere else, at least as far as I am aware. One was called the wall game and the other the field game. The former consisted of trying to push a ball up a wall and if one likes having one's face pushed into the mud and somebody else's studded boot ground into the back of one's neck then one would definitely enjoy it. I didn't play the wall game.

The field game* was quite a different matter. I considered it to be the best game in the world and the most boring to watch because nobody, except those who have attended Eton, understands it. I used to fancy myself at the field game and I even got my colours for it, which was probably the reason I was made captain of games in my house. My only other sporting achievement was winning the egg and spoon race in the house sports for four years in succession. That was done by cheating, with the aid of chewing gum, and not being caught out.

If you haven't thrown this book away yet, out of pure boredom, I really believe my experiences at Eton was a factor that helped me enormously when I was a director, and later chairman, of Ipswich Town. But more about that later.

*The following extract appears on the official website of Eton College: 'The Field Game is one of Eton's two brands of football, the other being the famous Wall Game. It is like soccer in some ways – the ball is round and a player is not allowed to pick it up – but the offside rules are more complicated (there being both horizontal and lateral offside) and there is also a scrum called a "bully". A team scores goals much as in soccer (although there is no goalkeeper), and one can also score "rouges" (rather like tries) and attempt to convert them. Seven players make up the bully, a "fly" plays behind the bully players (similar to a scrum-half) and there are three "behinds". Whilst the fly and the behinds generally possess greater footballing skill, the key to success lies with the bully players and their teamwork and fitness.'

One's In The Army Now

I WAS CALLED up to the army and joined a training battalion of the Welsh Guards* that was stationed at Sandown Park racecourse near Esher in Surrey. This was one of the most uncomfortable times I have ever had in my life but in spite of that I think it did me and a lot of other people, hundreds and thousands of them in fact, more good than anything else. If I didn't feel sorry for the army I'd have thought that national service would be a very good thing these days when you see so much ill-discipline around. In spite of that, I hope and pray like everybody else that anybody who is called for national service will never have to face a bullet in anger.

*The Welsh Guards was raised on 26 February 1915 by order of King George V to complete the national complement of regiments of Foot Guards identified with the countries of the United Kingdom. As a Foot Guards Regiment in the Household Division, the Welsh Guards are proud to provide the guard for Her Majesty the Queen at her royal residences. When carrying out these duties the Battalion is based in central London. The Regiment is currently based in Lille Barracks, Aldershot and comes under 19 Light Brigade. Mr John bucked a trend by joining the Welsh Guards as both his father and brother served with the Scots Guards.

When we first arrived at Sandown Park there was a draft of about 50 or 60 of us and we were put into what is known as a brigade squad. This was meant to be for potential officers. Sandown was not the ideal place for an army barracks but during the war there weren't many places that were suitable. The living quarters were rather primitive, to say the least. There were about 40 of us sleeping in double bunks in one of the Tote areas and our only washing facilities were in some loose boxes, which I was later informed had been condemned for use by horses. There was no such thing as hot water or any other so-called luxuries. There was another rather depressing notice at the gates into Sandown which read 'No Exit' and I promise that did nothing at all to increase one's morale.

The first thing that happened when we got into the camp or racecourse, whatever you would like to call it, was that we had all our hair chopped off into soldier-like fashion. Then we had to wrap up all our civilian clothes and send them home in a sand bag; one began to wonder if one would ever again wear a decent shirt or some comfortable underwear. After being a rather pompous, senior boy at Eton, a mere ten minutes of army life was enough to bring one back to earth with a real thump.

All of us being potential officers, it was obviously a marvellous opportunity for the trained soldiers, the non-commissioned officers and the sergeant majors to really take the piss out of us – and my God they made the very most of it. They chased us solidly from Reveille, which was about half past six in the morning, until lights out at ten o'clock at night. It was extraordinary in those days how some of the things one now takes for granted were so important then. I will never forget how one used to absolutely long, at about ten o'clock in the morning, for one's cup of tea, which used to be served in a large sort of billy can type of thing, already mixed up, and it really kept one going.

There is always something funny that happens and a very great friend of mine – I won't mention his name but he'll know exactly who he is if he happens to read this book – once asked a trained soldier if he could possibly have a little less milk and a little bit more sugar. Another great luxury of the day was a NAAFI break. We had one in the morning and another in the evening. Another friend of mine, on the very first day we were in the army, went up to the NAAFI and the nice girl behind the counter asked, "What do you want, mate?" He replied, "I would rather like some port and biscuits please," but needless to say neither was forthcoming.

One used to be woken up by the Reveille bugler at approximately half past six in the morning. Within 30 minutes one had to be fully dressed with boots polished, cap badge polished, all bits of leather polished, one's kit tidy and all one's bed made up. Then we were marched up to go and have breakfast. Shaving was the most difficult and painful chore – it was anything but easy with NAAFI razors and cold water.

For the first four weeks we were completely confined to barracks. In those days there was no film show and one's only luxury was the NAAFI. There were no sheets or pillow cases and we slept on straw pillows, which were far from comfortable. I was on a lower bunk and the person above me unfortunately used to dribble and suddenly in the middle of the night I would be woken up by this awful dribbling. I was very relieved that it was only dribbling!

The days consisted of extreme hard work. I was either being drilled or else I was being chased around the barrack square. By chased I mean people shouting at you to left turn, right turn, about turn, quick march, slow march, mark time, until I didn't really know if I was coming or going. There was one amusing incident when suddenly, in the middle of all this carry on, one of my mates just decided to sit down in the middle of the square, turned to the sergeant and said, "I'm terribly sorry but I just can't understand a word you're saying."

Weapon training, field training, assault courses, physical training, spit and polish, more drill, more chasing around, we did the lot. My God, at the end of those first four weeks, were we fit? A darn sight quicker than quite a lot of people who play football these days, I would say. It didn't take very long for a hangover brought upon by NAAFI beer to wear off. When the four weeks were over we were allowed out – my God, the luxury of being able to go to the cinema, talk to civilians, enjoy a glass of beer in a pub, sit in a moderately comfortable chair. It was absolutely marvellous. It just shows how much good it does to people and how it makes them appreciate the many luxuries they used to have, without really realising it, before they joined up.

After we left Sandown Park we were sent to Pirbright Camp, which is quite close to the village of Brookwood in Surrey. This was pure luxury compared to what we had gone through before. There was even hot water and showers, and we could also have a bath, while one of the really great things about Pirbright was that one could meet people from other regiments such as the Scots Guards, Welsh Guards, Irish Guards, all brigade of guards of all ranks. We all shared the same NAAFI and that is where I met and made so many chums from every single walk of life. I am very pleased to say that I still exchange Christmas cards with quite a lot of them.

I did have a slightly unfortunate experience whilst stationed at Pirbright Camp because every Sunday morning we had to put on our PT shorts and what were known as daps – they are called trainers today – before having to swab out our barrack rooms. I was swabbing away quite happily – okay, not all that happily – when I went outside to wring out my mop. There was a scream from the other side of the square, which appeared to be about half a mile away, and the next thing I knew I was being arrested by regimental sergeant major Brittain, who was very well known in the Coldstream Guards.

I was arrested and put inside. My alleged offence, I later learned, was urinating against the barrack wall. I tried in vain to explain that I was merely wringing out my mop but there was no getting away with it and my punishment was to be given three extra drills behind the gym. They took me behind the gym because it was well hidden away and they could really take the Mickey out of you and give you hell without anybody else seeing. That taught me a valuable lesson – after that I only used squeegees!

One of the things about leaving Pirbright and the training battalion was that one was promoted and made a guardsman. The next stop was the Royal Military Academy at Sandhurst, which was quite a different kettle of fish. Very tough going, but very good for you I would say, although there was still plenty of chasing by the sergeants and non-commissioned officers. One was called an Officer Cadet, but in reality we were called every single name under the sun, none of them complimentary. There was, however, a very quiet "Sir" at the end and that seemed to make all the difference.

During our time at Sandhurst we were sent up to north Wales to do a battle course, which mainly comprised going up and down Snowdon singing at the top of our voices. Our company commander in those days was a great friend of mine, although he was very much senior. Nowadays, Major George Fitzgerald is a neighbour of mine. We'd had a most marvellous war – several Distinguished Service Orders etc – and one day we were all going out on this battle course thing and he said, "I don't think we'll go out today because the weather is not good enough." In truth there wasn't a cloud in the sky. I have no idea what George had been up to the night before.

I had a slightly awkward moment when I was at Sandhurst, at the passing out parade. Being extremely bad at drill, not being particularly tall and obviously not a very good soldier, I was put right into the middle ranks, where I was hidden away from everybody else. There was some very pompous gentleman (possibly not actually pompous, but he certainly *looked* pompous) sitting on his horse taking the parade, and I can't remember who he was. Anyhow, the order came in for outward turn. I couldn't remember whether outward turn meant I should turn left or right, so I turned left and came nose to nose with my neighbour, who had turned the other way. We then both got into a total panic and turned round completely, and of course exactly the same thing happened on the other side. How in hell we got up those damned steps I will never know, but we had at least got our commissions.

About half a dozen of us were then sent out to join the first battalion in Palestine. We were about to take off from Liverpool but our departure was delayed. For some unknown reason our battalion in Palestine had a pack of three foxhounds, named Strawberry, Raspberry and Gooseberry. I think they used them to hunt jackal or hyena, but it isn't important. Soon after leaving Windsor Barracks we lost Gooseberry, who was last seen being pursued down the main road towards Reading by the regimental sergeant major on a motorbike. We eventually reached Liverpool to catch the boat, only to lose Raspberry, who was last seen heading rapidly towards the Mersey Tunnel. We finally made it into the troop carrying boat with just one foxhound, Strawberry, for company. The journey out there was fairly uneventful, although we did our best to get our knees brown. We didn't want to look too white when we arrived because we knew all our mates in Palestine would be boasting sun tans.

We eventually landed portside and amongst our luggage we had the Grenadier Guards' Christmas cards. Unbeknown to us, they turned the boat round in the middle of the night. We started to unload in the morning and unfortunately the cards were the first to go, landing slap bang in the middle of the Suez Canal. We were then taken to a transit camp, three to a tent, and we spent two nights there before we caught the train to Palestine. We still had dear Strawberry with us until early one morning one of the local Arab servants brought in some hot shaving water. The dog promptly sat in it, let out a piercing scream and the last we saw of him he was being pursued rapidly towards Cairo by one of my fellow officers, still in his pyjamas, in a trolley bus or tram. We never saw Strawberry again but fortunately my mate did turn up after searching in vain for the dog.

By this time both wars with Germany and Japan were over. Nobody was more pleased than we were to hear that the Japanese had surrendered because none of us fancied jungle fighting a great deal. Palestine was great fun. There were a few skirmishes going on – enough to keep one occupied – but it was such a fascinating country and well worth visiting in spite of the many problems we encountered.

I went back there with the football team in 1981 and went all over Palestine, and what the Israelis have done to that country is quite amazing. Having been out there for two and a half years, and bearing in mind it is not very big, I didn't recognise one single place. What used to be desert was fertile land, where there used to be camels and Bedouin tents was perfect farmland, with cows, pigs and sheep. They really have done a most remarkable job out there.

The St Moritz Years

HAVING COMPLETED MY national service and returned from Palestine, I joined the family firm of Cobbold & Co., brewers in Ipswich. I was sent on a brewing course down in Cheltenham, where there was and still is an excellent racecourse. Suffice to say that I didn't learn a great deal about brewing but I certainly did learn at a young age, about 21, that frequenting such places was a very expensive way of spending one's time. I became strictly opposed to gambling and to this day I remain very sad at the number of people who are parted from their money, a number of whom, I am sorry to say, play professional football.

After joining the family firm I decided that I would like to widen my outlook on life a bit. I have already explained what a complete failure I had been in all the sports I tried, so I arranged to visit Switzerland, where I had never been before, with the intention of learning to ski. That was a moderate success because eventually, after several years of trying, I did manage to get to the bottom of the mountain from the top without falling over too many times. I was much better, however, at the après ski and managed to perfect the art of lying in the sun at the top of a mountain and going back down again in the evening.

Talking about skiing, one of my better efforts was when I took along my brother-in-law, Roger Paul, and by the time we managed to get from the top of the mountain to the bottom it was practically dark. I was staying in the same hotel as they were and later that night I was summoned by a great roar from my sister. "Come upstairs immediately," she shouted in a tone of voice that made me aware I was in trouble. When I got to their room my poor brother-in-law was lying face down on the bed. The poor chap had sat down so many times that he had the pattern from his Aertex pants all over his arse! When all three of us met up for dinner, the daughter of the hotel owner came up to my brother-in-law and asked him where he had been during the day and what he had been up to. He quickly replied by pointing to the mountain through the dining room window and stating, "Up and down that fucking thing!"

I then decided that I would try to do something else, so I took to tobogganing and even risked life and limb by tackling the notorious Cresta Run in St Moritz. Let me stress, however, that this was in no way an act of heroism on my part. I was persuaded by a friend of mine that it was worth doing and that it was a recommended hangover cure. The very fact that one could rid oneself of a hangover in less than a minute and a half was all the encouragement one needed.

Now there is only one Cresta Run. It is made of ice and is about three quarters of a mile long. One goes down it in the traditional manner – head first on a skeleton toboggan with one's chin approximately four inches off the ice at speeds of up to 80 miles per hour. The total drop is more than 500 feet. It opens just before Christmas and closes again towards the end of February, about nine weeks in total, and it has been dubbed the ultimate thrill ride, far better than anything you will experience, for example, at Walt Disney World over in Florida. One's only way of steering was to move one's weight backwards or forwards, while braking was down to digging one's toe – the boots had little spikes on them – into the ice in order to slow down.

Riders who are out of control, which included yours truly more often than not, are certain to part company with their toboggan at the most famous corner on the run, Shuttlecock. Anyone who falls at this part of the run automatically becomes a member of the Shuttlecock Club and is entitled to wear the Shuttlecock tie. One particular visit to St Moritz springs to mind, when I fell so often that I was actually elected President of the Shuttlecock Club.

My preferred speed was probably around 50 miles per hour but on one particular occasion, when I was convinced that a corner went to the right but in fact it went to the left, I honestly believe I was travelling at a speed closer to 80 miles per hour. Needless to say, the toboggan and I parted company and I completed the final 100 yards or so flat on my face, which did nothing for my looks. They carted me up to the top and I was advised to see a dentist in order to put my jaw back into place and then a doctor to sew me up again.

The dentist I saw went under the great name of Herr Butcher and I understood why when he gave me an almighty whack in order to pop my jaw back into place. Next up was a visit to the doctor, who was called Herr Gut, and he proceeded to insert 30 stitches into the area above my top lip and on my chin. After the first two or three stitches I let out a loud yell and asked if he could give me some type of anaesthetic because it was hurting so much. "No anaesthetic," he barked, "because you will have less of a scar that way once it has healed." Personally, I wouldn't have minded a scar, as it could have been a talking point. I could have told my friends of my heroic act, which would have been utter nonsense of course, since my misfortune could be directly attributed to having had one or two wine gums too many the night before.

However, this little episode did at least work to my advantage. In those days foreign currency was very restricted, to the extent that one was only allowed to take about £25 out of the country and, as people can probably imagine, £25 didn't last very long in St Moritz. The reason I benefited from having so many stitches inserted in my facial wounds was that I had to take all my drinks through a straw. I've never been able to work out why it happens, but one drink consumed through a straw can have the effect of five or six drunk in the conventional way, which meant that I was able to save rather a lot of money.

St Moritz is, or at least it was in those days, one of the most fascinating places in the whole of the world. It was full of some of the most renowned people – like film stars and Greek billionaire ship owners – as well as poor people, like us Englishmen with our £25 pocket money. It also had some of the most fantastic parties to which, if one sucked up to the hosts sufficiently, one was occasionally invited. I remember once going down the Cresta Run and as I walked back up afterwards I spotted this very attractive girl standing on a platform on one of the corners. My friend and I immediately started to chat to her and much to our amazement she turned out to be none other than Grace Kelly*, the famous Oscar-winning actress from America who later married Prince Rainier of Monaco.

We were dressed rather like modern-day spacemen and she seemed interested in learning all about the Cresta Run. She was astonishingly good-looking and we suggested she might like to join us for lunch. To our delight she accepted and even agreed to go skiing with us afterwards.

We've made it at last, we were thinking to ourselves and then we set about wheeling and dealing, borrowing money right, left and centre so as to be able to afford lunch in the Palace Hotel**. She met us as arranged and was very pleasant company over lunch, but when we set off skiing in the afternoon, not only was it snowing but a fog and mist had also descended on the area and visibility was reduced to virtually nil.

We came to the conclusion that it would not be a good idea to go to the top of the mountain in such difficult conditions as we would have been skiing almost blind. What to do? Since no-one else was skiing, the bars and the bowling alleys were crammed full. Then I had a brainwave and suggested we visit the cinema, to which both my friend and Miss Kelly agreed. What should be showing but the Alfred Hitchcock film *Rear*

---

*Grace Kelly was born in 1929 and won an Oscar for Best Actress in 1954 for her part in *The Country-Girl*. She became Her Serene Highness The Princess of Monaco after marrying Prince Rainier in 1956. They had three children. She appeared in a string of major movies and alongside some of the industry's most popular male actors, including James Stewart, Clark Gable, Gary Cooper, Stewart Granger, William Holden, Ray Milland, Cary Grant and Bing Crosby, with whom she sang a duet 'True Love' in the musical comedy *High Society* that was to prove her final film after she decided to quit the business following her marriage. In 1982, a year after celebrating her 25th wedding anniversary, she was driving with her daughter, Princess Stephanie, when she suffered a stroke and her car plunged down a mountainside. She died in hospital the next day having never regained consciousness. Nearly 100 million people worldwide watched her funeral on television.

**Now known as the Badrutt's Palace Hotel, renamed after the family who launched the business in 1856 when Johannes Badrutt took over a 12-bed house and upgraded it into what is today known as the Kulm Hotel, the Palace Hotel celebrated its 110th anniversary in 2006. It was originally the St Moritz Hotel Beau Rivage until purchased by Johannes' son, Caspar, in 1883 and completely remodelled before being renamed and officially opened in 1896. It boasted Europe's first indoor tennis court in 1913, after which it became a regular haunt of the rich and famous, including royalty, wishing to engage in alpine sports.

Window in which she starred alongside James Stewart. Rather than putting her off, she said she had not seen the movie and so we settled down, my friend and I either side of her, to watch it. Not one person in the cinema was aware that the female lead was sat in their midst and we rather enjoyed the thrill of it all. The following day she flew back to America and that was the end of that.

St Moritz was the sort of place where you never knew who you would bump into next and I like the story, regardless of whether it is true or not, of the two men standing at a bar in London who were discussing the swish resort and what it had to offer. One said to the other, "Are you sending your wife to St Moritz this year?" and the reply came back, "No, I'm going to screw her myself this year!"

One regular feature of St Moritz in those days, and I imagine it still goes on, was the number of 'ladies' who used to offer their various services. This proved to be rather useful, although not in the way you might be imagining. They were paid in foreign currency – German marks, dollars, francs etc. – so they used to become a very useful way of supplementing one's meagre £25 allowance. I suppose one could have been had up for living off immoral earnings but we were always very honest and when we returned to England, where most of the girls were from, we repaid them in our own sterling.

In those days wigs were in vogue and most of these girls would wear them. I well remember sitting one morning at about 8.30am, rather frightened as I was about to embark on the Cresta Run, when a certain Frenchman, who owned a famous jewellery business in Paris, with branches in London, New York and all over the world, appeared. He was well known as a client of the girls and as he came tottering along he was sick outside the little hut I was sitting in. He entered the hut and in his broken English he told me, "Those blasted wigs, they get me into great trouble. Last night I gave the same girl two bracelets – what a waste!"

On one occasion a friend and I were walking up the hill when he suddenly complained of a very sore back. He was at a loss to explain how this had occurred. We messed about for most of the day before returning to our very small hotel. We never stayed at, or even went close to, the Palace Hotel unless there was a chance of a free meal or drink. We were having a drink at the bar in our very modest accommodation when my friend suddenly blurted out an explanation for his sore back. "You see that semi-circular sofa in the corner," he said. "That's where I screwed the barmaid last night!"

At the time I possessed a rather extraordinary woolly coat which achieved a certain notoriety, not only abroad but also in England. It was something I collected while I was stationed in Palestine, when I was bartering with some Arabs in an attempt to swap army blankets for eggs. For some reason I ended up buying two sheep. We ate the insides and I decided to wear the outsides. Obviously, the coat had a rather distinct odour – the skin had not been cured – but it didn't stop me wearing it when I was wandering about in St Moritz.

Every day when the Cresta Run came to a halt, which was usually around midday because the sun started to melt it, we all used to troop into a place called the Sunny Bar, situated in the Kulm Hotel, where we would sit on the veranda sipping our drinks. Eventually I decided it was time to totter back to my little hotel so I put on my coat and headed off. There were about 200 people on the balcony who saw me disappear down a little path when suddenly I was attacked from the rear by an Alsatian dog, which then tried to rape me. Fortunately, before I suffered a fate worse than death, it realised its mistake and ran off.

One of the great things about going to a place like St Moritz was that one met all sorts. Alongside some of the nicest people you could ever wish to encounter were some of the biggest shits in the whole of the world. This proved to be a great help later in life, sorting out the goodies from the baddies, those you could entrust with your life and those you couldn't trust as far as you could throw them. I must say I found it to be invaluable experience.

Political Failure

I AM THE type who will have a bash at anything. I even had flying lessons and I cannot imagine why. I had completed several lessons by the time my instructor and I were airborne above Ipswich one day. I was at the controls with him next to me and I successfully landed the plane. "You did that rather well," he said. "Now I'm going to get out so that you can take the plane up and fly around by yourself." I was having none of it, so as he got out one side I exited the other. I don't think I was much of a loss to the RAF!

As I record this tape I am sitting in the garden and it is open to members of the public. I have to say that I wish I could just tell them all to piss off, but I shall continue to tell you about my time in politics, which had played quite a major part in the family, both on my mother's and my father's side. My maternal grandfather was Victor Christian William Cavendish, the ninth Duke of Devonshire, and he became an MP at the age of 23. He was also Governor General of Canada and a cabinet minister in ... well, to be honest, I can't remember whose bloody cabinet. Also, an uncle by marriage, Harold Macmillan, was Prime Minister and another, James Stewart, was a cabinet minister. On my father's side, John Chevallier Cobbold, my great-great-grandfather, was a Liberal MP for Ipswich, so my own involvement wasn't a particularly new venture for a Cobbold.

I started off in 1950 when I became honorary treasurer of the Eye division of the Suffolk Conservative Association, which involved a considerable amount of work. In fact, it took up most of my spare time and it was rather like trying to get blood out of a stone. One had to go round to garden fetes and garden parties, even whist drives, and visit all the branches in order to raise valuable funds. People might be of the opinion that donations to the Conservative Party come from big business but I can assure you that in those days it was loyalty and hard work by a lot of dedicated individuals that was responsible for keeping it going.

I was then invited to stand in what was meant to be a fairly safe seat on Ipswich Borough Council. Unfortunately, I lost, but in my defence I should state that there was a very big swing towards Labour in that particular year and the reason behind me being asked to stand was that it was felt it would provide me valuable experience for the future.

At this point I wish to emphasise that I was not politically ambitious. I had no desire to become Chancellor of the Exchequer, which was just as well because I couldn't add up, and I definitely had no ambition to become Prime Minister. All I wanted was to represent and do my best for the people of Ipswich, who had done so much for my family and me during many generations. It was my home town and I would very much have liked to represent it in Parliament.

In 1955 I was adopted as the Conservative candidate for Ipswich. My opponent was a very well known Labour cabinet minister, Richard

Stokes, who was Lord Privy Seal and Minister of Materials, as well as being chairman and managing director of Ransomes & Rapier, a local engineering firm and probably at the time the largest employers in Ipswich. He had a fairly large majority and I was put in at a tender age just to learn what it was all about. Canvassing was a hard slog and I felt extremely sorry for those people who had to do it all. Well, not all, because I did a lot of it myself, but they certainly took the lion's share.

I shall never forget the count* for the first General Election that I fought against Dick Stokes. I was wandering round observing all the votes being counted and he came up to me and said, "Johnny, you're looking very worried. What's wrong?" I replied that my major concern, from what I was hearing, was that I thought I might win. Dick laughed and said, "Don't worry, the votes from a couple of housing estates are still to come in. I'll be alright and so will you." In the end I only missed becoming Member of Parliament for Ipswich by less than 4,000 votes, which I considered to be a very good result considering the electorate comprised some 82,000 people.

Had I been elected I would certainly have done my best for my constituents but I always thought it would have been like an apprentice on the shop floor going into work the very next day and assuming the role of managing director. In other words, in no way was I anywhere close to being properly qualified for the job.

Tragically, Dick Stokes was killed in a car accident in August 1957, so I was faced with a by-election. In a by-election one becomes the focal point of not only local interest but also on a national scale and I always

---

*Stokes polled 32,306 votes to Mr John's 28,724.

felt the experience helped me a great deal in the future as chairman of the football club. My opponent was Dingle Foot, a former Liberal MP for Dundee who became even better known when he defected to join the ranks of the Labour Party in 1956. This time I lost by a far larger majority* – about 7,000 I think it was – which wasn't really surprising since at the time there was a very big swing away from the Conservatives.

I went on to fight a General Election against Dingle Foot, who was later knighted, and on that occasion there was further competition from a female candidate representing the Liberals by the name of Manuela Sykes, a lecturer and graduate of London University who we nicknamed Little Audrey, after the American TV cartoon character.

I remember how, on one occasion, all three of us were on the same platform and I was batting last. I had a bit of a dig at the Liberals because two or three days earlier their leader, Jo Grimond, a great man in my view, had said that his party's aim at the General Election was to have 12 MPs in the House of Commons. My theme was that the election was not about electing 12 MPs but electing a government to run the country. At this point there was what I can only describe as a loud whisper as Miss Sykes said, "Don't forget, Jesus started with 12." As I had the microphone I should have been able to think of a clever answer but instead it was left to Dingle Foot, a QC and future Solicitor General, to come up with a classic remark delivered in a very loud voice to ensure that most, if not all, people in the hall could hear it. Turning to Miss Sykes, he said, "And who the hell do you think you are, the Virgin Mary?"

---

*Mr John attracted 19,161 votes, Dingle Foot 26,898 and Manuela Sykes 12,587. The Conservative vote fell by 9,563 but the next day a defiant Mr John vowed via a local paper, 'I shall stand again.'

In the 1959 General Election I was defeated again by Labour*, but by just a thousand or two thousand votes, and soon afterwards I was presented with a silver cigarette box by my local association. It was, I decided, a very good hint that they wanted someone else. I didn't blame them and to be perfectly honest I'd had enough of it by then. I removed my name from the list of candidates as I had no intention of ever again fighting an election anywhere, far less Ipswich.

Prior to my political career, if you can call it that, I had very little experience of public speaking. I had spoken at Licensed Victuallers Association functions but I always felt that one half of the audience were not interested in what I had to say, while the other half were too plastered to comprehend, so it mattered little what you actually said. Making political speeches was a different world altogether, since very few members of the audience, if any, were under the influence and people would hang on your every word. I had to change my mode of public speaking quite considerably. I might be wrong, but I doubt very much if a Licensed Victuallers Association audience would have been particularly interested if I had devoted my speech to the Suez or dollar crisis, or what we should do about the unemployed, of whom there were a great many less than there are these days.

It was bloody hard work, too, with every effort going into canvassing, visits to houses and three or four public meetings every evening. Canvassing should not only take place during election time if you are politically minded and fighting a marginal seat such as Ipswich took hours and hours of hard slog. I did it for seven years, between 1952 and 1959, and I

---

*Dingle Foot retained the seat with a considerably reduced majority of 3,215. Labour polled 41 per cent of the votes cast, Mr John for the Conservatives 36 per cent and Sykes 23 per cent.

should think I visited at least three quarters of the population of the constituency, as well as attending every type of event, from garden fetes to bowls matches and darts matches in local pubs. One local agent, a veteran of his type, told me, "I've never played so many bloody pianos in so many different bloody pubs!"

Having done so much canvassing, I quickly began to feel sorry for postmen because of the many different types of gate latches one had to undo and always remember to close again, along with the extremely hard springs on some people's letter boxes. Afterwards my hands were often quite literally black and blue, and on occasions minus a few finger nails, so postmen had my deepest sympathy.

Thankfully, there were always lighter moments and one concerned my dear mother, who worked like hell on my behalf. One day she was canvassing down a street and, being quite exhausted, I suppose she had lost her bearings. She knocked on a door and a very kind lady, immediately noticing that mother was slightly the worse for wear, invited her to come in and have a cup of tea. It was only after she had been in there a while that mother realised she was in the Labour Party committee room.

An elderly cousin of mine also joined my team to fight the by-election and it was her theory that one could tell people's affinity according to what was hanging on their washing line. By her reasoning, pyjamas belonged to Tories, night-shirts to Liberals and underpants signified a Labour supporter, although I decided it was not exactly a foolproof method of detection. The same cousin also had a rather unfortunate habit of stuffing literature through people's letter boxes if they did not answer the door. Before doing so, however, she would always write across the top: 'So sorry to have found you out.' She must have done this to thousands of houses before I pulled her aside one day to point out that her message, however well intended, had a double meaning and could perhaps cause offence.

Trying to become a Member of Parliament was all jolly good fun as far as I was concerned and I was helped by the fact that my political foes, Dick Stokes and Dingle Foot, were such good chaps. They probably regarded themselves as being extremely fortunate, too, since the candidate opposing them was someone they had every chance of defeating and, what's more, they did. We were all great friends and quite often stayed in the same hotel, where we returned after a hectic day on the road to have a drink. Before retiring for the night we would inevitably have a chat and decide what we were going to be saying to each other the next day. It was all conducted on a friendly basis, far more so than it seems to be today. As I say, it was hard work but also tremendous fun.

One of the great advantages of pursuing a political career was that I was able to meet so many people. On occasions it was quite embarrassing, especially if one encountered the same person for a second time. I remember approaching someone and saying, "How terribly nice to meet you. I haven't seen you for ages." He promptly put me firmly in my place by reminding me that not only had he seen me the previous week, but we had also had a lengthy conversation.

Of course, when I first stood for Parliament in Ipswich I was extremely raw and didn't really have much of a clue about what was going on. When I met Dick Stokes one day I decided to confide in him and ask if there was any advice he could offer. He told me, "Well, Johnny, at various meetings you will be asked a lot of questions and the chances are that from time to time you won't have the faintest idea what the answer should be. What you must do then is to turn to the questioner and say, 'What you really mean is this' and then ask yourself your own question. If you can't answer that then you really are in a muddle." From what I've seen on television, a lot of that is still going on these days and I have absolutely no regrets that I am not a part of it.

If I had become a Member of Parliament I think there is one word that would have summed me up pretty accurately and that word is wet. When I was a politician it was in the days of Messrs Butler, McLeod and Macmillan, who tried their hardest to make us one nation. That was my ideal and the reason I joined the Conservative Party. I accept that quite a few of the policies, although they worked temporarily, were not the answer in the long run. They appeared alright at the time but when the world recession came along they were, of course, inadequate and other stronger methods had to be gone into.

I was and still am a great supporter of the welfare state, but I think it has been overdone as well. It was a brilliant idea and RA – Rab – Butler, the Minister of Education in Winston Churchill's coalition government, whose Education Act of 1944 was a magnificent piece of legislation, encouraged the Tories to accept its principles. With hindsight, it was rather impractical to expect everybody to be looked after from the day they were born until the day they died.

My feeling is that there should be a standard of living under which no one should fall but everybody should have the opportunity to do the best for themselves, their family and, obviously, their country. If you go behind the Iron Curtain and you are not on an official delegation and try to look behind the scenes there is really no great difference. You still have tremendous privileges but you have got to be in the right position and the right place.

I remember when Ipswich played out in Leipzig and their officials, having been looked after very well when they visited us in Ipswich, were keen to reciprocate out in East Germany. One morning a large black limousine turned up at our hotel to transport me out to an official's home, which was on a par with some of the very grand stately homes you find in this country. I was greeted at the door by a butler wearing white gloves and I was given Russian champagne with fresh orange juice – good old Buck's Fizz, a very nice drink. I was shown around the magnificent house with fantastic furniture and paintings and he was very proud of his own private trout stream and also the woods, where he said that he and his chums shot pheasants.

That is not quite my idea of everybody in the state being the same and I cannot believe that a large majority of the people who live in the west would ever tolerate living conditions that exist beyond the Iron Curtain. There are some people in this country, thank God very few, who see it as acceptable, but I cannot accept that those people who have suffered it and continue to suffer it in Poland, Czechoslovakia, Hungary etc. would not, given the chance, prefer to have much more freedom and not have to suffer the terrible ruthlessness of the current regimes.

During the 1983 General Election, I personally believe that the Labour Party manifesto did more good for the opposition parties than for themselves. That was the reason for the enormous swing to the right. I think it is very sad that there is not stronger opposition to the Government and hopefully it will also be supplied in the future by the Alliance Party.

Many years ago, in conversation with Dick Stokes, he described politicians as a necessary nuisance. I think that is a very true statement. It seems to me an absolute nonsense that there are millions of people all over the world starving and yet in other areas there are what is known as mountains of butter and other foods, as well as wine. The answer is that someone far more intelligent than I am should be able to sort it out.

I am also very suspicious of religion, any type of religion regardless of where in the world it is practised. When one looks back over centuries of history it is incredible the number of wars, and subsequent loss of life, it has caused. It is still happening today – look at Northern Ireland – and I personally find it very hard to stomach that religion is said to bring peace on earth and goodwill to all men.

Joining The Club

FOR MANY YEARS, dating back to the club's formation in 1878, Ipswich Town was a very good amateur club and it wasn't until 1936 that it became professional and my father, who had been the prime mover in bringing the pro game to Suffolk, was invited to become its first chairman. In fact, it could be said that the professional club almost came about by accident. My father went to London one day with the intention of seeing one of his horses run at Alexandra Palace and beforehand stopped off to have a drink at his club, where he met a great chum of his called Sir Sam Hill-Wood*, who happened to be chairman of Arsenal.

Sir Sam apparently turned round and said to my father, "Ivan, don't be a bloody fool. You know your horses always come in last. Why don't you

---

*Sir Sam joined the Arsenal board in 1919, went on to become chairman and, like Mr John and his father before him, went to Eton. The Hill-Woods have been as prominent in the running of Arsenal as the Cobbolds once were at Ipswich. Sir Sam's son, Denis, was the Gunners' chairman and it is his grandson, Peter, an Old Etonian, who is currently at the helm. Peter Hill-Wood's home displays the famous photograph of Princess Diana, when she was a young nanny and a cameraman captured her in a long, see-through skirt. The child in her arms is his younger son, Charlie.

come with me and watch a soccer match?" My father said, "Not bloody likely. That round ball thing? No, not interested." But eventually ‑ I suspect it had something to do with the port or brandy, or whatever he was drinking – he was persuaded to go to Highbury and watch his first professional football match. From initially being opposed to the idea, he found himself enjoying it immensely and there and then he apparently made a promise to himself: *We're going to have this in Ipswich.*

Until then his only connection with the game was that he was president of the Suffolk County FA for two years before his appointment in June 1935 as president of Ipswich Town, who in those days were members of the Eastern Counties League and for whom professionalism was nothing but a dream.

When my father returned to Ipswich he set the wheels in motion and within a matter of months it had become reality. His chum, Sir Sam, provided plenty of encouragement and advice, even to the point of placing his London home at the disposal of the Ipswich board as they interviewed candidates for the post of manager. The first manager he appointed was Mick O'Brien*, who wasn't around very long before vanishing under rather strange circumstances. They were strange to me, at least, as a nine-year-old, but years later I discovered that the board had taken a dim view of his illicit relationship with a landlady of one of the brewery's public houses.

---

*Michael Terrence O'Brien was born on 10 August 1893 in County Kildare and died on 21 September 1940, aged 47. A central defender, he played for both Northern Ireland and the Republic of Ireland, and his many clubs included Norwich City before he retired from playing and was appointed manager of QPR in 1933. He joined Ipswich in 1936 and led them to the Southern League title in his first season in charge before departing in August 1937.

Lady Blanche Cobbold (1898-1987), Mr John's mother, was the first president of Ipswich Town from 1965 until her death. In February 1960 she performed the switching-on ceremony as the Portman Road floodlights were used for the first time when Arsenal were the opponents for a friendly match.

Captain John Murray 'Ivan' Cobbold (1897-1944), Mr John's father, was the man who introduced professional football to Ipswich in 1936 and was the new club's first chairman until his death.

Philip Wyndham Cobbold (1875-1945) joined the Ipswich Town board of directors in August 1944, two months after Captain Ivan Cobbold was killed, and succeeded him as chairman until his own death just 16 months later.

Major Robert Nevill Cobbold (1904-1944) was one of Ipswich Town's original directors when the professional club was formed in 1936 and was killed in action while serving with the Welsh Guards in Italy in May 1944.

Alistair Philip Cobbold (1907-1971) was Major Robert's brother and he joined the Ipswich Town board in February 1946. He was chairman between October 1949 and May 1957, when his cousin, Mr John, succeeded him. He remained a director until his death.

Mr Philip Hope-Cobbold, nephew of Mr John and the last remaining link between Ipswich Town, where he is Patron, and the family.

Mr John was the youngest chairman in Football League history when he took over as chairman in May 1957, aged just 29. Here he poses for a picture at a packed Portman Road, with the players' favoured mode of transport just behind him.

Mr John poses proudly with the League Championship trophy won by manager Alf Ramsey and his players in 1962.

Mr John, extreme right, became chairman as Ipswich Town were crowned Third Division (South) champions in 1957, pipping Torquay United on goal average. Manager Alf Ramsey, second left, joins players, left to right, Neil Myles, Ted Phillips, Roy Bailey, Billy Reed, John Elsworthy, Doug Rees, Ken Malcolm, Tom Garneys, Jimmy Leadbetter and Basil Acres at a civic reception to celebrate the club's success.

Mr John addresses supporters from the Ipswich Town Hall steps as skipper Andy Nelson and Ted Phillips show off the League Championship trophy won by Ipswich Town in a remarkable 1961/62 campaign, the club's very first in English football's top flight.

Mr John, drink in hand, chats with Alf Ramsey and goalkeeper Roy Bailey at a supporters' club party to celebrate the club's Third Division (South) title success in 1957.

October 1962 and Mr John congratulates Alf Ramsey on his appointment as England manager, a job he did not take up until April the following year.

Ipswich Town FC 1963-64. Back row, left to right, Jim Thorburn, John Colrain, Ted Phillips, Andy Nelson, Dennis Thrower, Roy Bailey, Jack Bolton, Trevor Smith, Jimmy Nelson, Dave Bevis. Second row, Stanley Prendergast (Assistant Groundsman), Roy Stephenson, Frank Treacy, Danny Hegan, John Smith, Noel Kearney, Doug Moran, Kenny Thompson. Third row, Jimmy Forsyth (Trainer), Ray Crawford, George Dougan, Bill Baxter, John Compton, Roy Walsh, Joe Davin, Ian May, Bobby Blackwood, Eddie Spearritt, Jimmy Leadbetter, John Elsworthy. Front row, seated, Willie Kerr (Director), Alistair Cobbold (Director), Major A D Terry (Director), John Cobbold (Chairman), Jackie Milburn (Manager), Cyril Robinson (Director), Wally Gray (Secretary) and Freddie Blake (Groundsman), standing.

An exciting new era in the history of Ipswich Town is launched in January 1969 as Bobby Robson arrives at Ipswich Station on his first day as the club's new manager. There to greet him was chairman Mr John, with Roger Nightingale (centre) ready to chauffeur them to Portman Road.

Mr John discussing heady Football League matters – or perhaps not – in 1973 with fellow chairmen George Reader (Southampton), left, and Denis Hill-Wood (Arsenal). Reader had previously been a referee and was in charge of the World Cup final between Brazil and hosts Sweden in 1950.

Ipswich Town 1973-74. Back row, left to right, Johnny Miller, Geoff Hammond, Peter Morris, Laurie Sivell, David Best, Kevin Beattie, Allan Hunter, Colin Harper. Front row, Bobby Robson (Manager), Ian Collard, Mick Lambert, David Johnson, Bryan Hamilton, Mick Mills, Colin Viljoen, Trevor Whymark, Clive Woods, Cyril Lea (Coach).

The day after the FA Cup final of 1978 and Ipswich director Murray Sangster, Mr John and Bobby Robson join the Mayor of Ipswich, David Myer, on the Ipswich Town Hall steps prior to a civic reception to celebrate the club's success in beating Arsenal 1-0 at Wembley.

Mr John and his brother, Mr Patrick, have canine company as they proudly show off the FA Cup.

Five members of the Cobbold family have become Chairman of **Ipswich Town Football Club.**

Capt. ' Ivan ' Cobbold – 1936 - 1944
Philip Cobbold – 1944 - 1945
Alistair Cobbold – 1949 - 1957
' Mr. John ' Cobbold – 1957 - 1976
' Mr. Patrick ' Cobbold – 1976 - 1991

In addition – Lady Blanche Cobbold was the Club's first President.

No other family has played such a key role in an English Football Club's history as

The COBBOLDS

Every picture tells a story and this one of a notice currently on display at Portman Road emphasises the huge part that the Cobbold family have played in Ipswich Town's history.

Portman Road 2009 and a stadium that bears no resemblance to the one Mr John knew as director and chairman in his early days on the board. But it is a lasting tribute to him that the transformation got under way during his period at the helm, most noticeably during the 70s and early 80s during Bobby Robson's time as manager.

Mr John was a club director when this picture was taken in the Ipswich Town boardroom in 1981.

Ipswich were then elected into the Southern League but it was always my father's intention that they should join the Football League. Another great friend of my father in those days was Stanley Rous and it was to him that he turned for advice once O'Brien had been dismissed and a new manager was required. Suffolk-born Stanley was immersed in football, first as a referee and then as an administrator, becoming secretary of the Football Association and then president of FIFA, the international ruling body. He was a good man to have on one's side, knighted as he eventually was for his services to football. He recommended that Ipswich should go after the Manchester United manager, Scott Duncan*, not just because of his football knowledge but because he felt he could be of great assistance in helping to secure precious votes from clubs in the north of England that would help to bring about Football League status for Ipswich.

The story of how Scott Duncan came to join Ipswich is that my father drove up to Manchester, put him in the back of his car and turned round to drive back to Ipswich. Upon his return he rang the chairman of Manchester United and told him, "We've got your manager and we're going to keep him – but there will be two cases of vintage port arriving in due course."

I don't like to discuss other people's salaries but I think it is pretty well known that Scott Duncan was extremely well paid. Indeed, he received

---

*Adam Scott Matthewson Duncan played for Dumbarton, Newcastle, Rangers, Dumbarton again, Cowdenbeath and Dumbarton for a third time before he was appointed secretary-manager of Hamilton Academical, Cowdenbeath and then, in June 1932, Manchester United. He won the Second Division title for United in 1936 but they were relegated the following season and he resigned to join Ipswich Town, who were then a Southern League side. He was instrumental in Town gaining Football League status in 1938 and he remained at Portman Road for 21 years, winning the Third Division (South) in 1954. He celebrated a testimonial in 1958 and returned to Scotland, where he died in 1976 at the age of 87. Of his 547 games in charge, Town won 223, drew 117 and lost 204.

more than any other manager in the country and on top of his £2,000-a-year salary he was promised a £1,000 bonus should he succeed in gaining the club admission to the Football League. With his many contacts in the game, he successfully canvassed on the club's behalf to gain entry into the Third Division (South) at the expense of Gillingham*, who failed to be re-elected.

An exciting new chapter in the club's history was under way and I remember how our first opponents were Southend United and that they made the journey to Ipswich by boat. Unfortunately, as everybody knows, the Second World War came along and everything was closed down. Virtually all the players went to various branches of the armed services and my father took it upon himself to settle all the club's debts, thus enabling it to make a fresh start once the hostilities were over. I cannot recall the exact amount but it was a considerable sum, around £11,000 I think, which was a lot of money at the time, but only enough to buy the left toe of one of today's star players.

During the war there were one or two friendly inter-service matches at Portman Road but that was about it. Scott Duncan gave up most of his contract, promised that he would carry on when the war was over, and went to work in Churchmans, the cigarette factory alongside the ground, before later taking a job at the brewery. In those days, of course, petrol was very, very strictly rationed, to the point where it was practically unattainable except for real necessities. One of those was mowing the Portman

*The only Kent club in the Football League, Gillingham returned 12 years after losing out to newcomers Ipswich and between 2000 and 2005 they were in the second tier of English football, achieving their highest-ever finish, 11th, in 2003.

Road playing surface, which Scott used to do himself, and that was only half of it because he also cut the practice pitch grass too.

Because of my father's death during the war my great uncle, Philip Cobbold*, succeeded him as chairman of the club but just a few months after the transitional 1945/46 season got us up and running again he too passed away and was replaced by Peter Chevallier**, who was managing director of Fisons and a very distant relation. Peter and Scott Duncan did something that I don't think anyone would dare to do these days by raising a considerable sum of money for the football club on the stock exchange. I don't think one's shareholders would really allow one to gamble in such a way.

Scott Duncan was a very cunning, crafty Scotsman. I wouldn't call him mean – that would not be fair – but let's say he was rather careful with the cash, both his own and that of the club. I remember on one occasion we were waiting at Waterloo Station in London, en route to a game in the south of England, when one of the players approached him and asked for a penny to go and have a cup of tea. "No," said the manager, "you pay for your own tea."

Another time we were having a drink at the Café Royal, during a break at a Football League meeting. Needless to say, I was paying for it, and sixpence fell to the floor. Dear old Scott must have spent five minutes on his hands and knees trying to locate the coin, which he eventually did, but when he got to his feet he was covered in dust. Not that he cared; as far as he was concerned it was a case of mission accomplished.

*Philip Wyndham Cobbold was chairman of Ipswich Town from 22 August 1944 until his death on 28 December 1945.

**Captain Peter Temple Chevallier was awarded a DSO and MC during the First World War, and was also a former Suffolk county tennis player. He was chairman of Ipswich Town from 5 February 1946 until he retired on 3 October 1949. He remained on the board until his resignation on 26 September 1950.

Scott thought of all sorts of ways of saving money. For example, when Tommy Parker, who held the record for most appearances until it was broken by another wonderful club ambassador in Mick Mills, joined the club direct from the Royal Navy he was put into digs at the local sailors' rest home. Scott told him he would soon make friends there but the real reason was to save a few pennies. I shall never forget the time I stuck my head round his office door and caught him in the act of watering down a bottle of whisky. I couldn't believe my eyes and asked what he thought he was doing. "Don't worry," he said, calm as you like, "it's only the referees' match-day whisky."

There are plenty of stories concerning Scott and I like the one about a player, Ron Trenter, who only played two first-team games for the club. He would have played at least one more had he not decided to visit the toilet about ten minutes before kick-off in a home game. When he returned to the dressing room he found an angry Scott Duncan waiting for him. "You're dropped," he said and Ron was also later to discover he was £3 worse off in lost wages.

Scott was superstitious and was always picking up hairpins off the ground, something to which the players soon cottoned on. When we were away from home they would head for the nearest Woolworths or any other shop selling hairpins – they only cost about tuppence for a box – and when Scott took the lads for their morning stroll they would scatter them at will. Poor old Scott didn't seem to cotton on and would go down on his hands and knees at regular intervals to scoop them up. Goodness only knows what he did with all the hairpins; he must have had a huge collection at home.

In terms of what he did for Ipswich Town, the club owes him a great debt of gratitude. I know how much he contributed to our entry to the Football League, utilising contacts at clubs all over the country, and in particular the north where he was extremely well known and liked, to secure their votes. But once we were there he also did a fantastic job on the football side of things. Not only did we become an established league club, he led us to the Third Division (South) championship in 1954, his penultimate season in charge.

There was a necessary change of chairman after Peter Chevallier retired and it was my cousin, Alistair Cobbold*, Philip's son, who took over. Scott, who was also secretary, had about a year of his contract still to run. Alistair decided we should start the search for a new manager and it was Nat Shaw, one of my fellow directors, who came up with the suggestion that we should approach Tottenham Hotspur because he had heard that one of their players, someone called Alf Ramsey**, was going to hang up his boots. Nat owned the Ipswich Greyhound Stadium and, believe it or not, the Ramsey family had connections with the sport and this was what made him aware of the player's situation.

---

*Alistair Philip Cobbold joined the Ipswich Town board on 5 February 1946 and was elected chairman on 3 October 1949, a position he occupied until 6 May 1957. He remained a director until his death on 8 November 1971.

**Alfred Ernest Ramsey achieved a unique football double. As a player he was a member of the Tottenham Hotspur side that in 1951 won the League Championship just a year after being promoted. He led Ipswich to the Second Division title in 1961 and in 1962 they won the First Division title for the first, and so far only, time. Ipswich also won the Third Division (South) crown in his second season in charge at Portman Road. He was appointed England manager in 1963, confidently declared that England would win the World Cup three years later and it was a promise he was to keep thanks to a 4-2 Wembley win over West Germany in extra-time. He departed in 1974 and largely kept a low profile for the remainder of his life. He suffered a stroke in June 1998 and died less than a year later in an Ipswich nursing home at the age of 79 after a heart attack. Of his 369 games in charge, Town won 176, drew 75 and lost 111.

Great Yarmouth had invited him to be their new player-manager, an offer he declined because he wanted to stay in League football, so it was agreed that we should contact Tottenham. We duly did so and we were given permission by them to speak to Mr Ramsey. I accompanied the chairman to the Great Eastern Hotel at Liverpool Street, where we met Mr Ramsey and discussed the possibility of him coming to Ipswich. Initially, we offered him the job of player-manager but he turned us down, stating that he wanted to concentrate on just one job and adding that it would be impossible to coach players who were also his team-mates.

We then revised our offer and said the job of manager was his if he wanted it. After some deliberating, he decided to accept our offer. However, he stressed that he also wanted to be secretary and he eventually persuaded the board of directors to appoint him in the dual role of secretary-manager. He also asked if he could be given time in which to prove himself as a secretary and to his credit, in a remarkably short time, he passed at least two of the chartered accountancy examinations, which I'm sure were far from easy.

It was a great achievement for someone whose entire career until then had been spent in professional football, so it was obvious he had spent a huge amount of his spare time studying for his exams. In the first year that Alf was with us there was obviously a certain amount of friction between him and Scott. I cannot remember how many times Alf offered his resignation, which was never accepted, and what happened in the future demonstrated that we were right not to do so.

Scott Duncan's last season in charge saw the club relegated back to the Third Division (South) but things improved virtually straight away under Alf. The team finished third in his first season, only missing out on promotion by one point, and the following year they won the Third Division (South) in dramatic fashion. Our last game was at Southampton, one of Alf's former clubs, and we won 2-0 but we then had an anxious wait to hear that our closest rivals, Torquay, had only managed a draw at Crystal Palace. So the title was ours and because we were booked into the Polygon Hotel – brother Patrick used to call it the Dead Parrot – I decided we would hold a party. I rounded up some street musicians and bribed the hotel pianist and violinist to stay on late.

The party was going with a real swing but when I went to find Alf I couldn't see him anywhere. Eventually I tracked him down, would you believe, underneath a table singing *Maybe It's Because I'm a Londoner*. Alf always hotly denied that this ever happened but I can assure you it is true. I can only assume that because of the state he was still in the following morning he had no recollection of it ever happening. We went on to gain further success, of course, as Alf's team – the credit could not go to anyone else – won the Second Division championship in 1961 and just 12 months later were crowned champions of the entire Football League, which is still being talked about today as a fairy tale and I am certainly not going to argue with that description.

Alf did a remarkable job, there is no doubt about that, but he was not one for showing emotion in public. He displayed a cold exterior, in fact, even upon the news coming through on the last day of the season from Burnley that they had been held to a draw by Chelsea, who had already been relegated. This meant that by virtue of our home win over Aston Villa* we

---

*Ipswich defeated Aston Villa 2-0 at Portman Road on 28 April 1962 thanks to two goals by Ray Crawford in front of 28,932 spectators.

were the Champions, the best team in the country. You wouldn't have known it by the impression on Alf's face, though. We had cracked open a case of champagne in the boardroom but Alf did not join us. He praised the players to deflect the attention away from himself.

The party had diminished somewhat by the time I finally discovered Alf sitting in the stand, looking out over an empty pitch. It reminded me of an almost identical situation a year earlier when we won the Second Division, but this time Alf did something different. We exchanged a few words and he calmly took off his jacket, handed it to me and I watched as he set off on his own individual lap of honour. The only problem was that the ground was deserted so the applause was missing. So while Alf, who was his usual immaculate self in collar and tie with black polished shoes, continued on his way I decided to provide the cheering and I kept it up until he returned to collect his jacket. Alf wasn't one to show his feelings in public but I felt privileged to share that very private moment with him and despite his rather dour public image I often saw a very different side of his personality.

On the back of his unparalleled success at Portman Road it was no surprise that Alf was sought out by the Football Association to become the next England national team manager, leaving us with the very difficult task of replacing him. We appointed Jackie Milburn*, a Newcastle legend and without question one of the nicest, kindest and most charming men ever to kick a football in the history of the British game. There was just one problem – Wor Jackie was most certainly not cut out to be a

---

*John Edward Thompson 'Jackie' Milburn was born on 11 May 1924 and died on 9 October 1988 at the age of 64. He was Newcastle United's all-time record goalscorer with 200 goals, until being surpassed in 2006 by Alan Shearer. He was a member of the Newcastle side that won the FA Cup in 1951, 1952 and 1955, and in 13 games for England he scored 10 goals. He was appointed manager of Ipswich on 29 April 1963 and resigned on 30 September 1964. Of his 61 games in charge, Town won 12, drew 14 and lost 35.

manager. I have always been very grateful to him, however, because while we did not get anywhere close to enjoying the success of his predecessor, and even came rather close to regaining the club its unwanted Third Division status, he started one very significant aspect of the club for which Ipswich has become renowned over the years and for that reason alone I regarded him as a success.

It was Jackie who got the club's very first youth policy under way. Ironically, it was something that we could never interest Alf in launching. Jackie, on the other hand, could see the wisdom of investing in youth and to his eternal credit launched a very successful scheme that continues to pay handsome dividends to the present day. Everyone at the club was willing Jackie to succeed in management, simply because he was such a popular and thoroughly likeable man, but it was not to be. When Jackie asked to retire I very nearly went on bended knee to persuade him otherwise. "No, Jackie," I would tell him, "you must give it another year." But eventually he was adamant that he was quitting. The situation was getting on top of him, he explained, and was even affecting his health and that of his wife, so I felt I had no choice but to let him depart. He returned to the north east, where he was quite rightly idolised for what he had achieved as a player for Newcastle, and it was clear when I next saw him, looking fit and healthy, that he had made the correct decision.

Jackie's departure led to us appointing Bill McGarry*, although only after I rather cheekily made an offer to Alf to return to his old job. I was

---

*William Harry McGarry was born on 10 June 1927 and died on 15 March 2005 at the age of 77. He played for Port Vale, Huddersfield and Bournemouth, won four England caps and managed Bournemouth, Watford, Wolves (twice), Newcastle and the Saudi Arabia and Zambia national sides. He guided Ipswich back to the top flight as Second Division champions in 1968 and of his 194 games in charge, Town won 79, drew 61 and lost 54.

serious but so was he when he declined, which didn't really surprise me because the job was only half done with England and he was not the type to walk away. Bill did a bloody good job for the club and the one thing we had in common was that I had just as extensive a knowledge of Anglo Saxon words and phrases as he had. When he used to let rip I could give as good as I took and we got on extremely well together. Bill took us back to the First Division, which was not easy, and we were glad to have him. It came as quite a shock, to be honest, when he announced that he was leaving to join Wolverhampton Wanderers. By his reasoning they were a bigger club and he was far more likely to achieve what he wanted to achieve as a manager with them. It was a personal blow that we lost him because apart from the on-the-field success he gained, Bill also advanced the youth scheme started by his predecessor and the club was in very good shape.

If I was shocked by Bill's departure I was to be even more shocked when, within a short time of him leaving, he was begging to come back again. "Please, Mr John, can I come back?" he said when we met by chance soon after he left. At first I thought he was joking but I quickly realised that he was serious, so unhappy was he in his new surroundings at Molineux. "I've got more bloody scouts than Baden Powell," I remember him telling me. Of course it was impossible to turn back the clock but I took it as a huge compliment to Ipswich that Bill had not found the grass to be any greener in his new location.

I well remember him arriving at Ipswich. I assembled all the players in the dressing room and took him in to introduce him. "This is Mr McGarry, your new manager," I said and without delay I turned on my heels and left. I later heard from the players that as soon as I disappeared through the door Bill had told them: "That was your fucking chairman and that's the last time you will ever see him in this dressing room." Perhaps Bill thought I might be the type to interfere but I think he very quickly realised that nothing could have been further from the truth. Indeed, it was the very first time I had ever set foot in the dressing room, but I don't suppose he was to have known that.

We chose Bobby Robson* to succeed Bill and this was after a strong recommendation from Dave Sexton, the manager of Chelsea at the time. He wrote me a very nice letter that convinced me Bobby was worth considering and I remember being accompanied by another director when I went to London to meet with Bobby. It was Bobby's honesty that shone through, from the look on his face and the way he talked to us. He had already been sacked by two clubs, Vancouver and Fulham, where he had

---

*Robert William Robson was born on 18 February 1933 and lost his brave battle against cancer when he passed away at his home in the north east on 31 July 2009, having beaten the disease on four previous occasions during the previous 17 years. He played for Fulham (twice) and West Bromwich Albion, and won 20 England caps, scoring four goals. He managed Vancouver Royals and Fulham before being appointed by Ipswich and of his 709 games in charge, Town won 314, drew 173 and lost 222. He led the club to success in the FA Cup in 1978 and the UEFA Cup in 1981, as well as runners-up spot in the First Division on two occasions. Having stayed loyal to Ipswich by rejecting a number of top jobs, he left in 1982 to manage England, leading them to the semi-finals of the World Cup in 1990, where they lost on penalties to West Germany. He then headed abroad to take charge of PSV Eindhoven (twice), Sporting Lisbon, Porto and Barcelona before returning home in 1999 to be appointed manager of Newcastle. He took them into the Champions League but was sacked in 2004. Awarded the CBE in 1990 and knighted in 2002, he was also granted the Freedom of Ipswich, Newcastle and Durham and in 2007, in an emotional ceremony, was given a lifetime achievement award duing the BBC's *Sports Personality of the Year* programme. In 2006 he was named as consultant to the Republic of Ireland international side under the new management of Steve Staunton, a role from which he resigned two years later. He dedicated his last years to the Sir Bobby Robson Foundation, which has raised over £2 million towards a cancer research centre in Newcastle.

been a very popular player, but I could tell that here was a man who would never let us down.

It is amazing what you can tell about a person so soon after meeting him. Bobby convinced me that he was the right man for the job, although I have to be honest and say that we had considered both Frank O'Farrell and Billy Bingham prior to me receiving the letter from Dave Sexton. He was employing Bobby to scout for him and sent him to a game at Portman Road, which fired his ambition to become our new manager. It was clear from our initial discussion that Bobby was a man of integrity, someone we could trust as long as we backed him to the hilt and kept faith in him, which is what I have always considered is the very least a manager should expect from his chairman and the board of directors. I also offered him a three-year contract, which again is the very least a manager should be given time-wise.

When Bobby had completed his first three years it was so obvious to us all in the boardroom that he was the man for us and so I offered him a ten-year contract. During that time he was approached by a number of other clubs, both English and foreign. All the approaches were conducted properly, within the rules, and I know for a fact that Bobby was tempted by some of the extremely high salaries being mentioned. He also knew, however, that we would do our damnedest to keep him and no matter how tempted he was by other clubs he always elected to stay put. We knew, of course, that if England came calling we would have to relent and that was precisely what happened in 1982.

Bobby's achievements are well known, but aside from winning the FA Cup he took us into Europe, almost on an annual basis, and we were the envy of many other clubs, hence the attempts to prise him away from us. I always regarded it as a great honour that Ipswich were representing their country in Europe and I have to say, also, that it was immense fun, travelling to different countries, seeing new places and meeting so many nice people we would never have encountered otherwise. Winning the UEFA Cup in 1981 was the icing on the cake, but our European adventures threw up all sorts of situations, most of them happy but with just one or two notable exceptions. In 1973, having finished in fourth place in the First Division, we qualified for the UEFA Cup and were drawn against Real Madrid. To the surprise of most people, given the Spanish club's reputation and past achievements, we won the tie and that saw us paired with the Italian club Lazio. We won the first game at our place 4-0, with Trevor Whymark scoring all the goals, and in the return in Rome we encountered what my uncle, Harold Macmillan, would have called a little local trouble. In truth, all hell let loose. The supporters burned the Union Jack and their players set about our lads at the end, with Bobby Robson managing to get them all in the dressing room, bolting the door and waiting for almost two hours before they felt it was safe to surface.

While Bobby and the players had a narrow escape, our Lazio counterparts could not apologise sufficiently for the behaviour of their supporters and players. Unable to return to our hotel because of the activity there and around the stadium – the riot police were called and it took them some time to establish control – we were whisked off to an extremely nice little restaurant just outside Rome, where the hospitality was first class. Not to put too fine a point on it, they entertained us right royally, although it also involved a slightly embarrassing experience for yours truly.

The wife of one of the Lazio directors, who I took to originate from Ireland, was undoubtedly an alcoholic nymphomaniac. Why did I form this opinion? Well, I was chased round and round a rather large pillar in the restaurant and fortunately managed to avoid capture. Eventually, having managed to keep her at arm's length, we had to lie on the floor of the bus with the windows firmly shut and the curtains drawn. Several bricks were thrown but fortunately there were no casualties and, nerve-racking as it undoubtedly was, I have to be honest and admit that it was far less frightening than the likely outcome had the director's wife been successful in capturing her prey.

Wherever we went in Europe we were always shown the greatest friendliness and afforded excellent hospitality. We were fortunate to play in many different countries and without exception we have had a great time in all of them. In the beginning, when Alf's team qualified for the European Cup, something my father could never have anticipated just 26 years earlier when he was chairman of the first professional club and they were members of the Southern League, our very first foreign assignment was in Malta. We won the game against Floriana 4-1 and because their ground had no baths or showers the team changed at their hotel. Our Scottish full-back, Ken Malcolm, had never even been in a plane before. He was feeling the heat – the temperature was in the 80s – as the match kicked off and about 10 minutes later he decided to wear a sun hat, which was something I had never seen before and have never witnessed since.

In the evening we were entertained to dinner by our hosts at a very pleasant restaurant in Valletta, the capital, and while it was an excellent meal our boys were clearly becoming impatient that it seemed to be taking an age to conclude the proceedings. I knew where they were headed – to a certain part of the town – and I have to confess I told a little white lie to speed things up. I persuaded our doctor to approach the president of the Maltese club and explain that the players, through not being accustomed to the sun and the heat, were extremely tired and keen to return to their hotel as quickly as possible and get to bed. The president went along with the request and wrapped things up fairly quickly, but of course the inevitable happened. We all piled into a bus and asked to be dropped off in the red light district. Within minutes, who should we bump into but the president, who laughed and said, "Ah, I could see through you. I thought I would find you down here."

One week later, Floriana came to Portman Road for the second leg and it was even easier for our boys, to the extent that we won 10-0, which remains a club record that I cannot see being beaten for a great many years, if at all. At half-time I asked the president if he would like a cup of tea and he said: "Don't be a bloody fool. I would like a proper drink, whisky, and make it a large one." I poured a generous measure and handed it to him, then a few minutes later I asked if he was coming to watch the second half. He looked at me as if I was mad before answering, "No, I am not. I am going to stay here drinking whisky." I plonked the bottle on the boardroom table and left him there on his own with it. Around 45 minutes later I returned to find the bottle empty and the president looking remarkably sober, although he clearly couldn't have been. He had every right to be proud of his achievement, which is no easy task and, having done it myself, or at least tried to, I speak from experience.

As I've said, our European adventures have been great fun, and if they hadn't been it would have been entirely our own fault. There's an American saying that comes to mind – life is like a sewer because what you get out of it depends on what you put into it. On our way to winning the UEFA Cup in 1981 we were drawn to play a Polish team called Widzew Lodz and it was heartbreaking over there to see the conditions in which people were living at the time. It was bitterly cold, snowing and the buildings were grey, making it a pretty grim spectacle. We saw people queuing for tiny bits of bread, butter and meat. It was not difficult to feel extremely sorry for them and I remember how our hotel was besieged with fans of the Polish club who admired English football and were keen to rub shoulders with our boys and collect autographs.

Bobby Robson had taken the sensible precaution of transporting a lot of our own food out there, which was common practice among football teams travelling behind the Iron Curtain. Apart from the steak and chicken that was to form the basis of our meals at the hotel, all the players were issued with several large bars of chocolate and lots of fruit, mainly apples, oranges and bananas. To their credit, the players shared their rations – chocolate and fruit were luxury items to the Polish people – with the locals who came to see them at the hotel. Indeed, some of the lads even gave away items of clothing, particularly pairs of jeans, along with music cassettes, to the extremely grateful locals. Needless to say, I was proud of the Ipswich players for their generosity.

As is the custom in Europe, the Widzew Lodz club hosted a dinner the night before the game and it was staged in our hotel, probably because it was the best place in town. We had entertained them to dinner and drinks at the Belstead Brook Hotel in Ipswich two weeks earlier and while they were keen to reciprocate I got the feeling they were rather embarrassed that they could not provide a meal to compare. I remember the main course was pigs' trotters and jolly tasty they were too. It was an excellent party, with both sets of directors and officials getting along splendidly, which is exactly how it should be.

The game was played the following evening and probably should never have taken place since the pitch was covered in several inches of snow, which had compacted in many areas. However, since we were leading 5-0 from the first game, and because the difficult conditions would hamper both teams, Bobby Robson agreed that it should go ahead. Although we lost by the only goal, therefore, we were safely through to the next round. I sat next to a charming gentleman who couldn't speak a word of English but we got along terribly well, due in part to a sort of sign language but mainly because he was only too happy to allow me regular swigs from his hip flask, which helped to keep the cold at bay, as did the large rug he spread across both our laps.

When the game was over he gave me a nudge, pointed to the pitch and said five words – "very good for Robin Cousins" – at which point we both burst out laughing. For those who don't know, Robin Cousins was a British figure skater who had won a gold medal at the 1980 Winter Olympics, in other words earlier that same year, and he would certainly have been far more at home on that pitch than any of the footballers were.

In certain areas of Europe one has to go along with local tradition and the one that has never suited me is where the host club separates the visiting president, or in our case chairman, from the rest of the directors. When we were in East Germany to play Lokomotiv Leipzig in 1974, for example, I was escorted away and plonked between two extremely large generals, the one on my left being Russian and the one on my right East German. They were covered in caps, rope and gold braid, and wrapped up in very heavy overcoats. Just before the kick-off the Russian general turned to me and without even attempting to lower his voice, making it certain that his East German counterpart must have heard, said, "I hope you beat these German buggers – we don't like them either!" Fortunately, and I cannot say whether it was due to him not understanding English or that he was simply being very diplomatic, there was no reaction whatsoever from the general on my right.

Another stop-off on our victorious UEFA Cup campaign of 1980/81 was in Prague, where we played the local team, Bohemians. We were very kindly invited to have lunch at the British Embassy, which happened to be the only building in the city centre that had been painted a colour other than grey. I happened to mention to one of the Czechs, who I knew could speak a bit of English, that I had a clever money-making idea, namely to return to Prague and open a paint factory. He was not amused and replied, "Don't be such a bloody fool, you would just be nationalised."

One of the club officials asked David Rose, the club secretary, and I to accompany him on a sightseeing tour of Prague and we readily agreed. It was a rather strange experience because it was conducted via the underground system. Whenever the train stopped at a station we would get off and clamber up all the steps to street level, have a look round, and then go all the way back down to the platform and wait for the next train. It was very tiring – we must have had about 16 stops – but at least we saw more of Prague than if we had been walking or even on a bus. I formed the opinion that with its tremendous bridges across the Vltava it was a beautiful city, although I still felt it could have done with a coat or two of paint.

When we qualified for the UEFA Cup for the very first time in 1973 our opponents were the most famous European team of them all, Real Madrid, with the first game at Portman Road. My brother, Patrick, and I went on the coach to Heathrow Airport to collect the official party and on the return trip back to Ipswich I sat alongside the Madrid vice-president, who spoke absolutely perfect English. When he realised our surname he surprised me by asking, "Are you related to Ivan Cobbold?" I said we were his sons and the Spanish gentleman said, "That is quite extraordinary. I used to know him very well at the beginning of the war and I used to supply him with cat gut to go salmon fishing. I also gave him a gaff for hauling the fish out of the river."

The vice-president, who we later established was actually a Duke, told us he was having lunch with our father in the Ritz Hotel in London when he handed over the gaff, which, quite rightly, is now an illegal instrument. It was a telescopic one and the Duke informed us that when our father opened it up he caught the wine waiter by the tails of his coat, which I thought was a rather novel way of ensuring quick service. When we flew to Spain for the second game the Duke – I'm sorry, I can't remember his full name – came to the airport to meet us and he gave Patrick and I a lift back to our hotel in Madrid. At the time Real had the famous German player Gunther Netzer in their team and as we were driving into the city the Duke informed us that Netzer was injured and would not be playing against Ipswich. "Nothing trivial I hope," said Patrick, who had a huge grin on his face.

When we played against Cologne in the UEFA Cup in 1981 we did the customary thing and took all their officials out to dinner at the Belstead Brook Hotel the night before the game. Patrick was then the chairman and in the middle of dinner he suddenly disappeared and came back two or three minutes later carrying a couple of rolled up newspapers. The President of Cologne was a very nice man, if rather serious-minded, and from what I can remember his company ran the national football pools, as well as operating casinos throughout the country. Anyway, Patrick made him play Are You There Moriarty? This is a game where two people are blindfolded and lie on the floor, feet to head, holding hands. In turns they ask, "Are You There Moriarty?" while also trying to hit the other person over the head with a rolled up newspaper. The game lasted about ten minutes and the other German officials looked on in amazement. When they finished the Cologne president told Patrick, "When you come to Germany we will play again and I shall put a poker in my newspaper."

We were fortunate enough to play against Barcelona on two occasions and it is a wonderful city. On one of the trips we had a group of supporters staying in the hotel with us and one of them – no names – picked up a rather elderly tart, only to discover that he couldn't quite match the asking price and was short by only about £1. He informed us of this the following evening and we told him that if he had told us at the time we would have had a whip-round for him. "No, I'm glad I didn't," he replied, "because when I saw her earlier tonight and I was sober I was relieved that I wasn't able to afford her."

After travelling as extensively throughout Europe as we have been fortunate to do in the last ten years or so, we have come to realise that the equivalent of our chairman is their president. My mother is the Ipswich club president and she is well into her 80s, and we always find it rather amusing that when foreign officials ask to meet our president they are somewhat shocked at the outcome. It's not really that surprising that so many foreigners don't really understand the British.

When we played against Aberdeen in September 1981 as we defended our trophy we found them to be one of the nicest, friendliest clubs we had ever come across. They deservedly beat us, there was no argument on that score, and we were the UEFA Cup holders at the time. Aberdeen were managed by Alex Ferguson in those days and it was always on the cards that he would come south and manage a bigger club. Knowing that Bobby Robson could well leave us to take the England job, as he did in a matter of months at the end of the 1981/82 season, Alex was someone whose name was mentioned as a possible successor and when Aberdeen defeated us over two games he was definitely a contender, someone we had in mind, although in the end we decided that Bobby's assistant, Bobby Ferguson*, had earned the right to step up after several years as a loyal lieutenant.

We had a change of venue when we entertained the Aberdeen officials the night before the first game at Portman Road. We switched the dinner to Le Talbooth at Dedham and the two sets of directors, as well as both managers, got along famously. It was the same up there and because brother Patrick was going to stay in Scotland on holiday after the second game he asked me if I would drop them a line. I was happy to do so and in my letter to their chairman, Dick Donald, I congratulated them on their victory, wished them every success in the remaining rounds and thanked them for their wonderful hospitality – the usual load of balls. I couldn't resist adding a PS that read 'What little I can remember I will never forget.' I was later informed that the letter had been framed and was hanging in their boardroom.

It is not really up to me at all to pass on advice to anybody, but I do strongly suggest to any football club fortunate enough to qualify for European competition that they should hold the official party before the

---

*Robert Burnitt 'Bobby' Ferguson was born on 8 January 1938 in Dudley, Northumberland, and started his professional playing career with Newcastle United before moving to Derby County, Cardiff City and Newport County, where he was player-manager. He accepted Bobby Robson's invitation to join the Ipswich coaching staff in the early 70s and later stepped up to first-team level. When Robson departed for the England job in 1982 it was to Ferguson that the board of directors turned as his replacement, although he found it difficult amid player departures and financial problems. Ipswich were relegated in 1986 and Ferguson relieved of his duties the following year. Of his 258 games in charge, Town won 97, drew 61 and lost 100. He spent a lucrative period coaching in Kuwait and later at Sunderland, after which he concentrated on scouting for a number of clubs, a role that sees him take in the majority of Town home games. He remains resident in Ipswich.

match and certainly not after it. This very sound piece of advice was passed on to me by the Arsenal chairman, Sir Denis Hill-Wood, after he had encountered exactly the same sort of problems with the Italian club Lazio as we later did.

It is difficult to say what has been Ipswich's best achievement – winning the League Championship in our very first season in the top division, bringing the FA Cup to Suffolk for the first time or joining the elite number of British clubs to have conquered Europe, which we did by winning the UEFA Cup. Mention of Europe, however, reminds me that my mother, our president, decided she would be present in Amsterdam for the second leg of the UEFA Cup final against the Dutch side AZ Alkmaar. She flew out on the day of the game and it was all terribly exciting for her. Her only concern as she departed was whether she would be kissed by the dashing Prince Bernhard, husband of the recently-abdicated Queen Juliana of the Netherlands, but luckily that episode did not arise. Mother left home at 5am and did not return until after midnight – not a bad effort, we thought, for such an old girl.

I would have to say that the League Championship represents the greater achievement, if only because it is such a long hard slog. To be precise, about nine months of solid work and endeavour by the manager, his staff and the players. At the same time, though, reaching the FA Cup final at Wembley was terribly exciting and I remember how Patrick and I, at the final whistle of our semi-final win over West Bromwich Albion at Highbury, broke our golden rule to avoid the dressing room at all costs. We simply had to congratulate Bobby Robson and the players at the earliest opportunity and I remember how we broke all the rules by lighting up in there to have a fag with Allan Hunter and Kevin Beattie.

Wembley was a wonderful occasion and although we were delighted to be entertained by the Football Association to a splendid lunch, I have to confess I would have rather been amongst our supporters enjoying the atmosphere. There is a story doing the rounds that my mother, who as President of the club was being entertained in the Royal Box suite, was invited to meet the Prime Minister, James Callaghan, who was a special guest for the match, and that she declined, adding, "I would much prefer a gin and tonic." That is not quite true because it was actually my brother Patrick, and not my mother, who made the remark. I want to get that one clear for the record books.

During the half-time interval at Wembley I went downstairs for a cup of tea, which I didn't really want. The truth is that I would have preferred something else to drink but couldn't find it. On coming back into the Royal Box the FA Cup itself was sitting there, with the red and white ribbons of Arsenal on one handle and the blue and white of Ipswich on the other. I must have had a premonition or something like that, because at that time the score was 0-0, but I removed the red and white ribbons and put them in my pocket just in case Ipswich didn't win. Fortunately we did, thanks to Roger Osborne scoring the only goal of the game, and the scenes the next day, as we made our way back to Ipswich having stayed overnight in London following our official banquet at the Royal Garden Hotel in Kensington, were quite incredible. We had a police escort, which we didn't really want as it meant we had to obey the speed limit, but practically from the moment we left the outskirts of London all the way back to Ipswich it was like a sea of blue and white on either side of the road, as well as on the bridges over it.

On the way home we all decided we were a little bit thirsty, although it certainly wasn't because we had not had enough to drink the previous night. We flashed the police escort in front of us that we wanted to call in at the Army & Navy pub in Chelmsford, which had become a regular stopping-off point on return journeys from London fixtures. The police realised what was going on and escorted us into the car park, which prompted Patrick to turn round and say, "I've often been escorted out of a pub, but never into one before, and definitely not by the police."

The reception we received upon returning to Ipswich and transferring into an open-top double decker bus at Portman Road was quite incredible. The police estimated that between 90,000 and 100,000 people lined the streets and crammed into the Cornhill in front of the Town Hall. For a town with a population of 125,000, that wasn't bad going at all. I was told afterwards that during the final, which was obviously televised live, there wasn't a single person to be seen walking the streets of Ipswich. I was also told that once the game had finished and people started to celebrate our splendid victory, they did so in the best possible spirits with no trouble at all. Indeed, I was told the police were joining in as the fans sang their hearts out and that is one of the great things about our crowd at Ipswich, who must be one of the very best in the country.

For the UEFA Cup final in Amsterdam we were cheered on by a travelling support of more than 10,000 fans, who made their way by plane and ferry from Suffolk. We received a letter a few days after we arrived back home with the trophy, to yet another open-top bus parade and civic reception. It came from the chief of police in the Dutch city to say that our fans were the best behaved crowd they had ever encountered in Amsterdam. That was great credit, not only to the people concerned but also to those who organised the many trips. We also received a similar letter from the people who ran the ferries saying that there was less damage caused as our fans travelled to and from Holland than there was on the normal crossings. We made a point of telling our local media and they reported the news, but we were sorry that it wasn't picked up on a national level because it was at a time when football supporters were attracting a lot of criticism and we were proud of the fact that our own followers were bucking the trend.

On The Board

QUITE A FEW of my mates, who were not the slightest bit interested in association football and in some cases thoroughly disliked the sport, often asked me what on earth I was doing being a director of a football club. They were even more taken aback when I became chairman but I told them then exactly what I had told them in the first instance – that it was hereditary. I will confess that I am not particularly keen on the game. I have said it many, many times and never tried to conceal the fact. Indeed, I remember saying that I would not cross the road to watch a football match – unless, of course, Ipswich Town were playing. When we won the FA Cup in 1978 it was only the second Wembley final that I had attended. The first one bored me to tears and if it had not been for a little sustenance in the restaurant beforehand I honestly think I would have caught an early train home.

Why, I often ask myself, is it that so many people want to become a director of a football club? Is it for the love of the game? Well, I sincerely hope so. I would not want to think it was down to personal prestige, a share of the limelight and an opportunity to project themselves or their own businesses. I would much prefer to think that someone who wants to join the board of a club believes they have something to offer the community, of which the local football club is usually the focal point, rather than seeking personal gains or – and here comes that awful word again – prestige.

What should be the responsibilities of a football club director? In my own personal opinion a director should be involved as little as possible. Directors, as in any other business, are responsible for the financial side of the club and therefore should be committed to keeping the books in a reasonable condition, while they should also seek to provide entertainment to a high standard, although that specific task should be left to the manager.

The two most important people at any club are the chairman and the manager, although not necessarily in that order. Indeed, having served as a football club chairman for nearly 20 years, I definitely consider the manager to be by far the more important of the two. It is the manager's job to manage, and with the minimum of interference from the chairman and directors. If he wants to ask advice, fine, but no manager should be given advice from anyone in the boardroom as to how his team should play football. Imagine, here at Ipswich, the likes of me, someone who has never kicked a ball in his life, trying to tell Alf Ramsey, Bobby Robson or any of the other managers we have had over the years, how the game should be played.

There are several million people in the country, among them a lot of football club directors, who think they could make really good managers. A large section of every club's support think they know better but they are all wrong. Here at Ipswich I hear people saying how lucky we have been with our managers, but it is not entirely down to luck. I have been fortunate in meeting all types of people throughout my life, which has definitely been an advantage, and while luck definitely has a part to play in football, we can honestly claim to have made good appointments based on our judgment.

Since Ipswich turned professional in 1936 we have never sacked* a manager, a record of which I am very proud. We had one who retired, Scott Duncan; we had one who resigned, Jackie Milburn; and we had one who thought the pastures in another field were greener, Bill McGarry, although he quickly realised this was not the case and regretted his decision to depart. Another two of our managers, Alf Ramsey and Bobby Robson, were pinched by the Football Association for the England international side and, once again, we are extremely proud to be the only club who can boast such a record.

Everything hasn't always gone according to plan. Yes, we've had our many successes, winning league titles and cups, but we have also been relegated on several occasions, although only once during my time as chairman. We wouldn't dream of sacking a manager just because we got relegated. We knew that the manager and the team were good enough to bounce back and that proved to be the case. I sincerely hope this will remain the policy in the future.

The most important thing for a director is to have a really good rapport with every single member of staff at the club, from the manager all

---

*Ipswich's proud boast that they had never sacked a manager ended in 1987, four years after Mr John's death, when the board of directors decided against renewing Bobby Ferguson's contract. His replacement, John Duncan, was sacked in 1990 and in December 1994 John Lyall resigned to be succeeded by George Burley, who was sacked in October 2002. Joe Royle took over but was sacked at the end of the 2005-2006 season and the job went to Jim Magilton, who was sacked by new owner Marcus Evans in April 2009 and replaced by Roy Keane.

the way down to the person who sweeps out the gutters. That relationship must exist and probably explains why Ipswich are so often referred to as a family club. It is no accident, but exactly how it was always intended it to be from the very beginning.

If one has favourites – and it is very difficult not to have favourites – one should never show it. Favouritism leads to jealousy, which can lead to an awful lot of trouble in all walks of life. My personal problem when I first joined the board was how to be addressed. I was opposed to Sir and didn't even want to be known as Mr Cobbold. As far as I was concerned both sounded rather old-fashioned and pompous, so we eventually arrived at a very happy compromise and I was known as Mr John, which I think suited the bill, and that led to my brother being known as Mr Patrick, which was fine by him too.

It is also very important for directors to get to know the players at the club, whether it be the most junior apprentice, the most senior professional or the club captain. I always took pride in knowing them and their families, and would talk for hours with some of them about everything bar football. It meant that I got to know them as men, as individuals, and understood them a lot better. I have learned to be discreet, too, after club tours abroad. Sometimes, I must admit, I and one or two of my fellow directors also hoped that the players might have been a little more discreet as well.

One thing football club directors should not do is get involved in the playing side. I have known directors to frequent the dressing room, while some have regularly undertaken scouting missions, but I very quickly learned my lesson on getting involved. It was definitely not my idea, but when I was on holiday in Scotland I received a telephone call from Scott Duncan and he asked me to go and watch a Stirling Albion player. I agreed and set off in my Land Rover to drive the 50 or 60 miles to Annfield, their charming ground, whereupon I introduced myself and explained I was a director of Ipswich Town.

We have always been proud of the hospitality we offer at Portman Road but Stirling Albion had a marvellous system of almost covering the boardroom table with small glasses full to the rim with whisky. It represented a generous dram and I have to confess that I had several. Upon returning back to my house in Perthshire I wrote out a full report and sent if off to Scott. Three or four days later I received a very curt telephone call from Scott in which he explained that the player I was supposed to be scrutinising had not even played. I had clearly disregarded the team changes and have never been scouting since.

Looking to the future of football, it is going through a difficult time at the moment but I must say that in my view the game has brought a lot of the difficulties upon itself, and I am prepared to take some of the blame myself. I do not personally agree with the concept of what they are calling a Super League because I think we already have one, namely the First Division, and I would not like to alter the structure at all. What I think is most important is that all clubs have an opportunity to get into the top division. Had such an opportunity not existed, where would Ipswich Town be? We have been through the lot.

I well remember being invited by Arsenal to attend a gala dinner celebrating the fact that the club had been members of the First Division for 50 years, a great achievement and I think I am right in saying they are the only club to have achieved it. I congratulated them on an absolutely magnificent record, but to my way of thinking Ipswich have done even better. We spent 25 years going through every bloody division, rising from the bottom to the top, and let no-one forget it.

When one talks about the decline in soccer in general, in no way can one blame the players. If any club is foolish enough to go and pay £1 million-plus for a player, of course he is going to demand his pound of flesh. Who wouldn't? I think it would be a tragedy if English soccer was dominated by half a dozen clubs, the big ones who attract the biggest gates. Things in this world have got to move on and the encouraging thing is that these big clubs cannot possibly monopolise every player in the country. As for wages, everybody has to get together and try to control the situation and I think there are signs that this is beginning to happen.

The system of promotion and relegation must continue but I can see massive problems ahead for the smaller clubs. I know people have been saying it for years, and very few clubs have actually gone out of business, but I think the time is rapidly coming when I am afraid a lot of them are going to have to drop out of the Football League. I don't think that need be the last we see of them, however, just as I have never considered being relegated with Ipswich as the end of the world.

I can also see a lack of finance forcing clubs to revert to part-time players, while I think it would make sense for the lower levels to be more regionalised, therefore cutting down on travelling expenses for both the clubs and their supporters. I know the Third and Fourth Division clubs are against this idea but I don't see any other alternative if they are to stay afloat. As for the big clubs, I can see them going into a European League, especially as it is just as easy to fly over to Europe as it is to travel the length and breadth of this country.

The most important people in professional football are the spectators and we must never lose sight of that. They pay the players' wages and are entitled to expect to be entertained. Some managers and coaches pay too little attention to this and have actually removed a lot of the excitement from the game. How I would love to see players like Stanley Matthews or Tom Finney, charging up the wings, taking on defenders and, more often than not, leaving them in their wake. Where are the great goalscorers, the modern-day equivalents of Tommy Lawton, Jackie Milburn and, in our own case here at Ipswich, Ray Crawford and Ted Phillips, who used to think that scoring less than 30 goals each meant it had been a poor season?

The language of football has even changed for the worse. What is wrong with calling a centre-half a centre-half instead of a sweeper, who in my book is someone who goes up a chimney? And why are forwards called strikers, who I thought were people who sat outside factory gates when there is a dispute on? The position they play seems to have nothing to do with the number on their back – why? They may be trying to fox the teams they are playing against, I have been led to believe, but surely the opposition can't be as stupid as all that.

Football needs more forward, attacking play. There is nothing more boring than to see the ball being passed backwards and sideways. That is not the way it is meant to be played. I think the people largely responsible for changing the game, and for the lack of wingers, were the Hungarians, who defeated England 6-3 at Wembley in November 1953 and 7-1 in Budapest six months later, two performances that made people sit up and take notice. Okay, it succeeded for a short time but then other people cottoned on and, with the greatest of respect to the Hungarians, no-one can claim that they have reigned supreme in the world since that moment.

I think it would be very nice, not to get rid of the individual skills of the players, but to bring back some of the more old fashioned styles of play. I know this puts me at risk of being called an old square, but while I am old I am not square. Actually, oblong would be a more accurate description. I don't want to give the impression that I'm an old misery. I admit I'm not a perpetual optimist but I believe there is a great future in everything worked for and encouraged. It is no good going around with a long murmuring, 'Fings ain't wot they used to be!'

One's object in life should be to make people happy and have a good laugh. Most importantly, one must be able to laugh at oneself. Have a good giggle and enjoy life as much as you can. As I said right at the beginning, I was born lucky and throughout my life – I've got no intention of finishing it yet – I've always done my best to help my fellow human beings, providing as much entertainment and amusement as possible along the way.

It occurs to me that instead of 'I' it should be 'we' in a number of places throughout this book, particularly with regard to Ipswich Town, which has always been a happy, united club and which I sincerely hope will continue to be so for the duration of its life. This has been achieved not by one person alone but by the combined efforts of everyone privileged to have served on the board and as club officials.

Bits And Pieces

NOW WE COME to a section I think we will call Bits and Pieces. I shall warn you now – there are one or two four-letter words used. I think swearing in general entirely depends on the tone of voice you use. If one really wants to give somebody a rocket I don't think one should use foul language. My idea of using four-letter words, and sometimes possibly more letters, is as a term of endearment and there are certain stories one hears that would be absolutely ruined without them and so the last thing one wants to do is offend people. I am a big fan of limericks and we often used to have a competition on the team bus to see who could come up with the best one incorporating the name of a football team and preferably the team we were travelling to face.

This is the first limerick I ever heard – I should think I was about 12 or 13 at the time – and to my horror I found myself reciting it one day as part of a speech I made to a rather serious mixed gathering at an Aston Villa Football Club luncheon.

There was a young lady from Coleshill
Who sat on the top of a mole's hill
The resident mole
Stuck his snout up her hole
Miss Coleshill's alright but the mole's ill

I assume my love of limericks, and my sense of humour generally, came from my father. During the war, when there was obviously a great fuel shortage, he penned a little rhyme which he sent to the Ministry of Fuel and Power. It read as follows:

If it's cold for your desire
Poke the wife and not the fire
If you live a single life
Poke the other bugger's wife
Poke his wife and poke your own
But leave that bloody fire alone

Father was most disappointed – and even offended – that his rhyme never appeared in print. He thought it would make a great slogan to be plastered on walls and billboards to encourage people to limit their use of fuel.

A few years ago our close season summer tour was to Barbados and one evening a small group of us – myself, Patrick and two players who shall remain nameless – paid a visit to Harry's Bar, which was quite well known in those days. It was a real disappointment. The place was very scruffy, all we could find to drink was rather warm Coca-Cola and there were two naked black girls rolling about on the floor together. We sat there for a short time and nothing seemed to be happening so we decided to get up and go somewhere else. At that point one of the girls sprang to her feet and said, "Don't you want fucky fucky?" One of the players quickly replied, "No, I want homey homey, taxi taxi, quicky quicky."

Another summer trip took us to Martinique in the Caribbean and we were staying in a very nice hotel. Close to the swimming pool a middle-aged woman was lying sunbathing and she was completely in the nude. She was very close to the pool and all the boys were having a look every now and then. Eventually she moved a bit further away and one of the players said, "Thank God for that – I hope the flies go with her."

The hotel had its own casino and one of our players, Eric Gates, who I'm sure won't mind me revealing his identity, was doing extremely well at blackjack. Eric loved gambling and he was doing so well that as he won more money in the form of chips he was getting other players to go and cash it in for him, as he daren't leave the table. The croupier was a giant of a man and every time he won a hand Eric would say, "Got you again, you big black bastard."

The money kept rolling in and Gatesy must have repeated himself at least half a dozen times. The croupier remained straight-faced, said absolutely nothing and just continued to deal the cards until Gatesy decided he'd had enough and left with his profits. The very next day we were playing a game against a local side – nothing too serious, more a way of helping to subsidise the cost of the trip – and you should have seen Gatesy's face when he realised that one of the opposition defenders was the big black croupier. It was quite a laugh to see Gatesy trying to keep out of his way throughout the game for fear of being clobbered.

Many years ago we were playing in Blackpool and I was the only director to travel with the team. I decided to go for a wander and I saw a sign outside a bar advertising champagne at half a crown per glass. I went in and purchased a glass and how they ever got away with calling it champagne I shall never know. When I came out there was a chap sitting in the gutter and he was trying to sell a monkey for a fiver. Well, I just had to buy this monkey, which was wearing a collar and lead, and when I took it back to our hotel you can probably imagine the reaction from the players. I took it with me on the coach to the ground and went into the boardroom at Bloomfield Road, where I introduced it as Ipswich Town's newest director, adding that it had only been appointed about an hour and a half earlier. At that point the blasted monkey slipped its collar, shot across the tea table, upsetting several cups, and charged out of the window. I've never seen it since and it had obviously been well trained by its owner, who had probably profited in exactly the same way on several occasions. As a money-making scheme I thought it was ingenious.

I love this joke and have decided to include it for precisely that reason. There was a married couple who lived up in Scotland and the husband was very hen-pecked by his wife. He was sent down from Glasgow to London to do some shopping and one of the things he had to buy was an ironing board. He managed to find one and took it with him on the 7.30pm train from Euston. He was in a first class sleeper and in those days there were four bunks, two up and two down. He was in one of the top ones and just as he was about to go to sleep he turned over and saw a very pretty girl on the top bunk opposite him. "Ahoy there," he called out, "how would you like to come over here?" The girl said she would absolutely love to but queried how she would get across from her bunk to his. "Don't worry," said the chap, "I've got something here that's about five feet long so you can come across on that." At that point there was a cry from the bottom bunk of, "How is she going to get back?"

During and just after the war every Sunday it was the custom when one was in the army to have regular church parades. There was one that took place in the Guards Chapel, which at the time, because it had been bombed and had still to be rebuilt, comprised nothing more than a Nissen hut. The only thing left was the altar and the guardsmen were marched in by the colour sergeant major. They all lined up and took their seats in the various pews. The colour sergeant major went up to one of the men and ordered him, in all seriousness, "Take your hat off in the house of God, you c**t."

That reminds me of an incident when Bobby Robson and Patrick were sitting together at the airport in Barbados as we were all waiting to fly back to England. A large Jumbo jet suddenly landed and Bobby said, "I wonder where that came from." Patrick replied quick as a flash, "Out of the bloody sky, you great c**t!"

Bermuda was another of our ports of call for a close-season club trip and one morning all the players were sitting round the pool when my brother Patrick joined them. He asked one of the lads, "How are you feeling this bright morning?" The player yawned and replied, "Bloody knackered and if you want to know why, she is sitting just behind you."

I was in my club in London many years ago and there was an old boy, not someone I knew, standing at the bar having a drink. Another chap came in and thrashed him hard across the backside with his walking stick. "Hello, you old turd," he said. "Are you still living with my wife?"

Now for another absolutely true story. It happened during the war to a great friend of my parents as he was walking back to his flat in London. It was late at night and his journey took him through Shepherds Market. He was accosted by a tart who said, "Would you like a bit of fanny dear?" The chap replied, "My God, does it come to pieces?"

Talking of tarts, a famous English Duke, who is now dead, was wandering down Jermyn Street in London when he approached one. "Have you ever been screwed by a Duke?" he asked. "No luv," she replied, at which point he said, "Well, you're just about to be." I could name the Duke, but I don't think that would be fair.

I remember we were playing a certain First Division club at Portman Road and after the match I was having a drink with their chairman. He obviously hadn't realised that I was a bachelor because he asked me, "You must be away a lot. What does your wife think when you get home?" Luckily, I thought fairly quickly and replied that I had no trouble in that area, adding, "She licks me all over and shits in the passage." He looked at me rather strangely but I disappeared and went to my car, where my spaniel was waiting. I returned to the boardroom with her and went up to the chairman and said, "Meet the wife!"

Many years ago, on a bitterly cold day, we were playing against Nottingham Forest and Alf Ramsey was our manager at the time. It was a particularly boring match – even I knew that – and suddenly a Forest player put the ball past his goalkeeper for an own goal. Our supporters were clapping and cheering, but not a word, not even a murmur, from Alf. I turned to him and said, "Wake up, Alf, we've scored a goal." He answered, "Bloody cold, isn't it?" I think it was the only time I ever heard brother Patrick give anybody a rocket when he said, "Alf, concentrate more on the game and less on the weather!"

I used to fancy myself as a driver of fast motor cars. I bought myself a TR2 – that will make you realise how long ago this happened – and I decided to enter it into a race at Snetterton long before it became a proper race track. I took part in the race and by the time I completed my last lap they had even started to take down the beer tent. I may have fancied myself as a driver, but no-one else did and I have to confess I was also had up for driving under the influence. As I had only had my driving licence back for 18 months after being banned for the self-same offence it was all rather embarrassing and I was advised by my solicitor to go for trial by jury.

So along I went and my defence counsel was somebody called Michael Havers, who later became MP for Wimbledon, Solicitor General in Edward Heath's government and Attorney General when Margaret Thatcher was Prime Minister. He was also knighted and one of his sons, Nigel, is a well-known film, stage and television actor who I remember accompanying his father to Portman Road on a number of occasions when he was my guest. It was suggested that I should go to a jury because I hadn't hit anything but someone had hit my car.

It was long before the days of the breathalyser. Michael was cross-examining the inspector from the police station where I'd been carted on the night in question and he asked him, "How well do you know Mr Cobbold?" The inspector said he knew me extremely well, at which point Michael asked, "When he was brought into the police station did he appear to be drunk?" The inspector immediately replied, "Not at all, just his normal self." I wasn't quite sure how to take that one, but after escaping a prison sentence I decided I would take no more risks. Did I stop drinking? No, I came up with a far more sensible solution and employed a chauffeur.

A good friend of mine was walking up St James' Street in London when he fell over. I think a matchstick had got in his way. Anyhow, a policeman came along, picked him up and dusted him down. Smelling his breath he said, "I think you're rather drunk sir." My friend replied, "Of course I am. I don't fall over when I'm sober."

This may surprise a lot of people, but I used to have a rather romantic side to my life. Indeed, there was a time when I thought I had fallen head over heels in love with an extremely nice girl. Unfortunately for me, but luckily for her, I was turned down, although that may have had something to do with my method of proposal, which I think put her off. It was on platform one at Paddington Station just as her train was pulling out and reflecting on it afterwards I suppose I could have chosen a more romantic location to be rejected. Another romantic side to my life was when I caught crabs in a first class sleeper going through Darlington. One never knows where one might catch something.

Not very long ago my brother Patrick and I were having lunch with the Ipswich Town manager, Bobby Ferguson, in the Centre Spot restaurant at Portman Road. We were discussing the pros and cons of capital punishment. Bobby said that instead of hanging criminals he would castrate them. I perked up and said that wouldn't get rid of them but Bobby answered, "Maybe not, but by God it would make them squeal."

I was having a drink one day with a friend of mine, George Leeds, at our club in London when in came the Duke of Bedford, who introduced himself with the words, "I'm Bedford." George naturally replied, "I'm Leeds." He has since hotly denied that story but even if it is untrue I regard it as well worth repeating. One of my great beliefs in life is that one should never spoil a good story with the truth.

Many years ago my mother was president of the Suffolk branch of St John Ambulance and every year she would host a weekend course at her house, Glemham Hall. It was a very large house and between 70 and 80 people would come along for the lectures etc. A lot of them were in sleeping bags on the floor and it was a source of great amusement when mother showed us their names. There was a Mrs Bugg, a Mrs Smelly, a Mrs Germy, a Miss Leech and a Mr W C Pile. The course ended, apparently, with a talk from Mrs Smelly on the subject of hygiene!

My mother once had a letter from somebody saying that she would no doubt be very sorry to hear that Mrs Davies had died. My mother thought that Mrs Davies must have been the widow of our former gardener. The letter also included information about the date and time of the cremation so along went my mother to the service, where she was rather surprised not to recognise even one single person. Afterwards my mother went shopping in Ipswich and came face to face with Mrs Davies, the gardener's wife, so to this day she has absolutely no idea whose funeral she attended.

There is a story about the late Duke of Gloucester, when he was colonel of the Scots Guards, going out to visit the regiment when they were stationed just outside Cairo. After dinner some of the officers decided to take him to a nightclub and there were one or two belly dancers performing the cabaret act. After they finished one of the officers turned to the Duke and said the usual form was to invite the girls to join them at their table. The Duke gave his approval and when the girls arrived there was a deathly silence. An officer suggested to the Duke that he should say something to them, whereupon he turned to the half-naked belly dancers and asked, "Do you know Tidworth?"

When I was standing for Parliament in Ipswich we organised a mass meeting in the largest hall we could find in the town and it was crammed full of between 800 and 900 people. They didn't all come to hear what I had to say. The main attraction was the appearance of Rab Butler, the Home Secretary, who very kindly agreed to speak in my support. At the time he had recently pushed through the House of Commons his street offences bill, which was designed to rid the streets, mainly of London and the other major cities throughout the UK, of the many tarts who used to accost people. Mr Butler explained the thinking behind his bill to the large audience, stating that prostitution was the oldest trade in the world and that it would be well nigh impossible to get rid of it altogether. He added that there was nothing more sordid than to be walking along the street of any large city with your wife or girlfriend and to be approached by one of these women. "I have taken the line," he concluded, "that it would be far better if it was driven underground." At that point a voice from the back of the hall shouted, "Another bloody shaft to the miners I suppose."

We were playing in Holland on one occasion when a very staunch supporter, who was based in the same hotel as the official party, suddenly disappeared in the middle of the night, obviously with only one intention. I saw him at breakfast the next morning and asked him, "Did you have a good screw last night?" He was rather hard of hearing, or at least he pretended to be, and replied, "It's raining in Diss!" Not to be undone, I repeated the question until he understood exactly what I was on about and he finally answered in the affirmative. We were in Rome a couple of years later and the same gentleman came with us, once again departing from the hotel in his usual way. When I bumped into him in the morning, before I could get a word in, he said, "It was like a thunderstorm last night." There was no answer to that, I decided.

There is a story I heard many years ago and which I have absolutely no reason to presume is anything but wholly true. It concerns my late grandfather. After his wife had produced their sixth child she told him, "Victor, that's it, no more children. You must make a visit to the chemist's shop." My grandfather tottered off and upon entering the shop and seeing another customer he decided he could not ask for the particular item he wanted to purchase. So instead he bought two tins of Andrew's fruit salts. He had no idea what they were but when he got home he swallowed the whole lot and couldn't understand why he had such an upset tummy for about a week. Grandfather was also very keen on cricket and at one time was president of Derbyshire Cricket Club. After attending a meeting he wrote in his diary, 'Went to a cricket meeting in Derby – fun; missed train to London – tiresome; went home – boring.'

Well, that's it, and I hope you have not found this book boring.

What They Said About Mr John

WHEN JOHN COBBOLD passed away in September 1983 the tributes poured in from far and wide, but none was more poignant than that of Bobby Robson, the former Ipswich boss and England manager at the time, who said, "Mr John was like a second father to me. His death is untimely; he was too young and too good to die and it is a sad and heavy blow to me. His death is also a dreadful loss to the club. He could turn disappointment and disaster into humour and laughter. That was one of his great attributes. There was always tomorrow as far as Mr John was concerned.

"If every club had a director on the board like Mr John, football generally would be in a better state. As chairman, which in my opinion is the number one position in a club, he was the most ideal and perfect man to work for. He was, in fact, my motivator and I just felt I had to succeed for him."

Fate, in the form of an unemployed Robson successfully applying at the tail end of 1968 to be the new manager of Ipswich, intervened to team him and Mr John together. "The electricity flowed," said Bill McGarry's replacement as Town boss, but only after Billy Bingham and Frank O'Farrell both declined Mr John's invitation to take charge.

Sir Bobby – he was awarded the CBE in 1990 and knighted in 2002 – recalled how Mr John startled him over the proposed construction of a new stand at Portman Road. Although badly needed because the club only had seated accommodation for a mere 1,800 spectators at the time, Ipswich were not prepared to endanger their financial health and it was a topic that split the six-man board. "Your decision, then, Bobby," said Mr John, handing the manager the casting vote. Bobby, wisely as it turned out, opted to build and by the time it opened, and again when it was extended a couple of years later, every single seat in the stadium was sold as a season ticket. The stand in question, by the way, is currently known as the Cobbold Stand. There was an action replay years later when demand for tickets again well exceeded Portman Road's capacity and the only solution was to build a new stand, then known as the Pioneer Stand but more recently re-christened the Britannia Stand.

'There will never be another John Cobbold and I still miss him,' wrote Sir Bobby in his autobiography *Farewell but not Goodbye*, while recalling a classic incident that occurred one day in the Highbury board-room as Arsenal prepared to take on Ipswich. 'With kick-off rapidly approaching, the Gunners' chaplain said, "Come along now, Johnny, may the best team win," and Mr John replied, "Fuck that, Reverend, we want to win."'

In an interview in the *Sunday Times* on 24 July 2005, Sir Bobby elaborated on his relationship with Mr John, adding, 'John Cobbold, he was a special breed. They've thrown away the mould for that type of guy; you don't find him in modern football. Basically, he knew nothing about the game and never interfered one iota, just gave me loads of support and guidance. When we won, he never bothered me, but when we lost, he would ring on Sunday morning and say in his Etonian stammer, "Bbbbbbb, Bbb, Bobby – are you all right?"

"Yeah, fine, Mr John. Just fine."

"Bbbbbb, Bobby, I would love you and Mrs Robson to come out to my place. We could have a bit of lunch."

"That would be lovely, Mr John," and Elsie and I would go there for lunch, but only when he felt I needed a little support. Over that lunch he would sympathise and say, "It wasn't our turn yesterday. But we have given the other team the pleasure of winning."

'I was so competitive and would wonder if Johnny was for real. But he was one in a million. The nearest any club comes to that kind of attitude today is Arsenal. They still have that bit of breeding, that class, reflected in the Hill-Wood family. Peter, the son, is a marvellous chairman. You never see him in the paper, do you, making big statements? If Arsène Wenger is going through a tough time with results, they are at their best, the whole board, including David Dein. One of the pillars of the game, Arsenal.'

Arsenal had a particularly close relationship with Ipswich during Mr John's time as a director and chairman, thanks in the main to the fact that his father, Captain Ivan, was a close personal friend of Samuel Hill-Wood, who was chairman at Highbury between 1929 and 1936, and again after World War II between 1946 and 1949. It was after he accepted Mr Hill-Wood's invitation to attend a first-team fixture that Captain Ivan returned to Ipswich and immediately forged ahead with plans to bring professional football to the town. Just as Captain Ivan was succeeded at Portman Road by Mr John, a similar situation occurred at

Arsenal with Samuel being followed in the role of chairman by his son, Denis, and from 1982 to the present day his grandson Peter has been at the helm – all of them, like Mr John, Old Etonians.

In the book *Football Gentry* by Brian Scovell, Arsenal chairman Peter Hill-Wood recalled how he was invited to be a guest at Mr John's home, Capel Hall. 'It was a very good night. He [Mr John] brought out a large bottle of whisky and the only thing was that he left the French windows open and the donkeys, Alka and Seltzer, kept wandering around the house. He didn't mind.

'By ten at night I was pissed and suggested we should have something to eat. "Great idea," said Johnny, "let's see what we've got in the fridge." I followed him into the kitchen and he opened the fridge door to reveal half a bottle of fresh orange and one egg. "Ah well," said Johnny, "let's get another bottle of whisky opened!"

'We went together on trips to Europe to attend European draws. Once we were in Monaco and he invited every member of his board and we were well represented. Our delegates went to the function to see the draw being made but the Ipswich party remained in their hotel drinking. They didn't know the draw until we got back.'

At the time of Mr John's death, Peter Hill-Wood said, "We value a long-standing friendship with John Cobbold. We always enjoyed Ipswich-Arsenal fixtures – John made sure of that. We will miss, but never forget, his infectious sense of fun. Football has lost its finest ambassador."

There has never been a stronger chairman-player relationship than that which existed at Ipswich during Mr John's 19 years at the helm and virtually everyone who served the club has a favourite story to tell. Captain at the time of Mr John's passing, Paul Mariner, who had joined the club from Plymouth in 1976, also paid tribute to him after his death, recalling how he had signed for Ipswich almost seven years earlier and his very first meeting with Mr John.

He said, "When I first came up to Ipswich with my wife Ali we arrived at the ground feeling apprehensive and not knowing what to expect. Bobby Robson met us and introduced us to a jovial man called Mr John, as we all knew and loved him. The first thing Mr John did was to go straight over to Ali and welcome her to Ipswich, completely ignoring me. Ever since that first meeting he always enquired about Ali before asking how I was. That's the sort of man he was.

"What I most admired about him was the way he had time for everyone at the club and in terms of the playing staff he made an effort to go and see the reserve and youth team fixtures, instead of completely focusing his attention on the first-team lads as I know is the case at other clubs. I know how much this meant to the younger players who subsequently joined the first-team squad and Mr John's terrific example created the happy atmosphere that prevails throughout Portman Road.

"Mr John was the main reason why the club enjoyed such a marvellous reputation throughout Europe and he is going to be sadly missed. Indeed, it will take a while for us to accept and realise that he is not going to be around any more. On behalf of everyone on the playing staff, I want to express my deepest sympathies to the members of Mr John's family. I know they will understand when I say we all considered ourselves to be his second family."

A touching tribute was paid by Aberdeen chairman Dick Donald after the two clubs – the Dons were managed by Alex Ferguson at the time – struck up a close friendship after being paired in the UEFA Cup just two years earlier. He said, "Obviously, Mr John was a tremendous character and will be a loss to football in general. He treated the game the way it was intended – for fun and entertainment – and his death is personally felt by the Aberdeen directors and management as they thought of him not only as a football colleague but as a friend."

Similar sentiments were expressed by Sir Arthur South, the Norwich chairman, who said, "As a football chairman, he stood out like a jewel. His leadership and standards set were a model for us all. He will long be remembered and we are all the poorer for his passing." Another tribute was paid by Everton chairman Philip Carter, who said, "John had that rare quality of camaraderie to which everybody responded. He will be missed most of all for his enthusiastic welcome and constant good humour. We at Everton feel privileged to have known him and count him as a friend. Football in general will be poorer for his passing."

Journalist Bob Oxby of the *Daily Telegraph*, whose sports editor eventually banned him from Portman Road for his own good, wrote, 'The loss of John Cobbold will mean that the town and football will never be the same again. No longer will teams leave Portman Road with a warm glow, despite having lost. When the boardroom was dispensing its legendary hospitality, only one subject was barred from the conversation. Even Bobby Robson, either elated by victory or dejected by defeat, was told, "Don't come in here talking about football. Let's have fun!"

'It was my privilege to be a friend and guest of Mr John on countless occasions over 20 years. He would pretend to blow his nose on my tie and refuse to laugh at my jokes (his were better). Once he claimed that my doctor had barred me from Ipswich on health grounds. It was a story that deserved to be true because, as my wife will testify, I usually slept through *Match of the Day* after a trip to Portman Road.

'In an age when the true lover of the game worries about the type of people who are taking control of football clubs, Mr John, his brother

Patrick and the rest of the board shone like a good deed in a naughty world. Mr John will be impossible to replace, both as a football man and as a friend, but his example has set a pattern to follow for those who have the destiny of soccer's friendliest club in their hands.'

The game's ruling bodies were also quick to add their tributes. Football League secretary Graham Kelly, later chief executive of the Football Association, wrote, 'I would like to underline the great loss, not only to Ipswich Town Football Club but to the Football League and the game in general. Mr John was a remarkable character who epitomised all the values we hold dear in football. He was the one person to whom results were not everything.' In a joint statement, Football Association chairman Bert Millichip and general secretary Ted Croker wrote, 'It was with much regret that we learned of the death of John Cobbold. He had an incredibly sensible outlook towards the administration of a Football League club and had a wonderful relationship with both Alf Ramsey and Bobby Robson, which enabled Ipswich Town Football Club to achieve one of the most impressive records in the history of League football. His sensitive feelings towards any subject he dealt with were appreciated by all those around him who were, inevitably, friends. The exceptional facilities at Portman Road, for a relatively small club, will be a lasting testimony to his leadership.'

The Ipswich manager at the time of Mr John's death was Bobby Ferguson, who devoted a large part of his programme notes for the home game against West Bromwich Albion on 24 September 1983 to paying his own personal tribute. He wrote: 'Mr John was a wonderful man and it is impossible to put into words the terrible loss that we as a club and, indeed, football in general has suffered. It is equally impossible to describe a character such as Mr John. He had a marvellous nature and while football is a game of emotions he hated to see anyone looking or feeling sad. He made it his job to pick people up and he was a terrific motivator.

'Mr John wanted to win as much as anyone – but he wanted to do it in the right way. And the way in which he accepted defeat was a lesson to us all. He was a unique person in the world of football, someone who always had the interests of the game and his club uppermost in his mind. Being a club director was no ego trip for Mr John; he served with integrity and honour but always in the background. Quite simply, he is irreplaceable.'

Former Ipswich player and first-team coach, Bryan Hamilton, met Mr John on the day he signed for Ipswich in August, 1971, initially without realising it. He was holidaying in Chester when he received a phone call from Billy Bingham, his manager at Irish club Linfield, telling him a deal had been agreed with Ipswich. Hamilton, who later managed his country and also returned to Portman Road on two separate occasions as first-team coach, recalled, "I met Billy in London and we caught the train out to Ipswich to meet Bobby Robson at Portman Road. We spoke for a while in his office then I nipped downstairs. A chap was sitting there having an ice cream and he asked if I wanted some. He seemed very pleasant but I replied, 'No, thank you, sir' and went back up to Bobby's office. When Bobby and I had agreed everything he told me the chairman was coming along to meet me. I couldn't believe it when I was introduced to Mr John – the very same fella who had invited me to share his ice cream!" That was just one of many amusing stories featuring Mr John that Hamilton, who also had a spell as manager of Norwich City, incorporated into a speech he delivered during a period on the after-dinner circuit.

Scottish winger Frank Brogan had a similar experience seven years earlier, having arrived to discuss a proposed transfer from first club Celtic to Ipswich. He was only 21 at the time and, he admitted many years later, he was by no means certain he was doing the right thing, despite the fact that a fee had been agreed between the respective clubs. He was in manager Jackie Milburn's office and remembered, "Jackie and I were sitting there, chatting away, when this chap appeared in the doorway. It was the summer, but he was wearing a heavy tweed suit and scuffed brogues. His tie was loose and his shirt collar askew.

"Jackie stood up and introduced him to me. It was John Cobbold, the chairman, and within seconds I knew I would be signing for Ipswich. I'd been five years at Celtic and our chairman, Sir Robert Kelly, hardly spoke five words to me in that time. But Mr John couldn't do enough for me. He spent an entire day with me, showing me round the area. He bought me lunch and I was fascinated by him. He impressed me no end. My life was enriched for having known him."

If Mr John had a rival as a practical joker, it was Ted Phillips, the scorer of 181 Ipswich goals en route to Third Division (South), Second Division and First Division titles, who had a vast repertoire of tricks he delighted at pulling at the expense of others. Phillips and Mr John were chatting one day when the chairman challenged him to take to the field wearing a long ginger wig and there was a considerable sum of money at stake by way of a wager.

Phillips recalled, "I was up for it straight away and I can even remember we were playing Leicester at Portman Road. The reason I know that is because they had Gordon Banks in goal. Anything for a laugh, as far as I was concerned, plus Mr John promised to pay me a few quid. I stuck it on in the dressing room and I could hear people saying,

'Who the hell is that?' as I ran out with the rest of the team. After the game Mr John duly paid up and we had a good laugh about it.

"As everyone knows, Mr John loved a drink," Phillips continued. "You could hear him before you saw him because he had so many whisky miniatures in his coat pockets. When we won at Tottenham on our way to winning the First Division it was regarded at the time as the best result in the club's history. Spurs were the Champions and it meant so much to Alf Ramsey as he had been a player at White Hart Lane. After that game Mr John insisted we go into the first pub we came across, which was right outside the ground. It was full of Spurs supporters but we went into the posh bit, the lounge, and there was no trouble. Mr John bought the first round. Alf didn't like the way Mr John would take the players for a drink but he could do nothing to stop him."

Another member of the title-winning side of 1962 was centre-half and captain Andy Nelson, who said, "Mr John will be remembered with great affection by all those who knew him and not least for his ability to find a laugh in any situation. He often said he knew nothing about football but he played no small part in creating the magnificent club that Ipswich is today. It was also Mr John who appointed, and more importantly allowed to develop, two England managers. Football today can ill afford to lose the likes of Mr John."

David Johnson was a major hit after joining Ipswich from Everton, so much so that he was capped by England and then returned to Merseyside, this time to join Liverpool, where he went on to enjoy further success, at home and abroad, with Bob Paisley's all-conquering side. He also holds an Ipswich record – the first, and so far only, player to halt a board meeting – which he did in the wake of the 4-0 UEFA Cup win over Lazio in October 1973, when strike partner Trevor Whymark scored all Town's goals. Johnson had been stretchered off in a great deal of pain after a horrific tackle from a vengeful opponent caught him in the most sensitive of areas. He spent two nights in Ipswich Hospital and upon his release, rather than return home, he instead decided to visit the club, where he found a board meeting was in full swing. The boardroom door was open for ventilation purposes and the directors caught sight of Johnson as he went past. He remembered, "Mr John got up from the head of the table and came out into the corridor to see me. He asked how I was and I said, 'I'll show you if you like.'

"I waddled into the boardroom and produced the evidence. I unzipped and popped it on the table and there were a few winces. I said it had given a whole new meaning to the phrase off-the-ball tackle and they all cracked up. Mr John said, 'Bloody hell, you need a transplant!' and I replied, 'Not from any of you buggers, thank you very much.'

"It was typical of Ipswich and I can't imagine it happening at another club. I'd moved on to Liverpool by the time they won the FA Cup in 1978, but I just had to be at Wembley to see the final, even though I was on crutches at the time because of another injury. I couldn't have been happier for Mr John and everyone else even if I'd been in the side. And the funny thing is that the FA Cup was the only trophy I didn't win in my career."

Jack Bolton was one of a number of Scottish players to take the road to Ipswich in the Sixties during Jackie Milburn's ill-fated spell as manager. A centre-half, he didn't enjoy any on-the-field success during almost three years, but he laughed when recalling, "My time at Ipswich was the best of my career. I saw the Beatles there and I met Mr John, someone I could never forget because I always knew I would never meet anyone like him no matter how long I lived.

"He was an amazing character and I was invited out to his home several times. I remember the night Mr John, me, Danny Hegan and Joe Davin rowed out to the lighthouse off Felixstowe. We must have had three cases of whisky on board. The keepers were pleased to see us and we were in no hurry to leave!"

Former Ipswich goalkeeper Ken Hancock, who made 180 appearances between 1964 and 1968, remembered how the squad was rewarded for avoiding relegation to the old Third Division with a Mediterranean cruise for themselves and their partners. "Poor old Mr John," recalled Ken. "The trip was his idea but for some strange reason he was allocated a cabin right next to the engine room and he was so hot that by the first night he'd had enough.

"The swimming pool seemed a good place to cool down but it was only half-full and they had slung a net over it to stop people using it. You should have seen the looks on people's faces when Mr John turned up with a blanket and pillow, jumped on the net and shouted, 'Goodnight everybody!' Some of the guests were tut-tutting away, full of airs and graces. But long before the cruise finished Mr John was the most popular guy on board – the life and soul of the party."

Years later, striker Frank Clarke also played a leading role in saving Ipswich from the drop, this time from the top flight. He and Scottish winger Jimmy Robertson were signed by Bobby Robson, from QPR and Arsenal respectively, at a total cost of £90,000 in March 1970 and their arrival triggered an upsurge in form that saw Town bank nine points from a possible 14 to climb clear of the relegation places. Clarke remembered how he and Jimmy were part of a club trip to Spain when Mr John approached the pair and offered to buy them a drink.

"We both asked for a soft drink," recalled Frank, "but Mr John said, 'Have a pint.' We explained that the manager would definitely not want us to be drinking but Mr John said, 'He won't say anything in front of me' and promptly ordered two pints."

Clarke, one of five brothers to play professional football, also remembered how he asked the club for a £3,000 loan when he moved to Portman Road and how Mr John not only agreed but provided a personal cheque. "When I moved on to Carlisle in 1973 I wrote a cheque and took it into him. He said, 'What's this?' and when I explained I was repaying my debt he said he'd forgotten all about it. I'd only been at Carlisle a short time when I received a letter from Mr John. It was lovely, very touching, and I've kept it all these years. It is one of my most treasured possessions."

Ipswich great Kevin Beattie has two outstanding memories of the fun-loving Mr John, whose antics enthralled players from other clubs when they were regaled by the Town star over dinner during international get-togethers. "At first," recalled Beattie, "I think the other lads in the squad might have thought I was making up the stories. But then after a while they – and I'm talking about major stars like Kevin Keegan, Peter Shilton, Alan Ball and Trevor Brooking – would come up to me at future squad meetings and ask if I had any more yarns to tell them. They couldn't believe I was talking about the chairman because he was unique, not the least bit like the people who ran their clubs.

"I'll never forget the night over at his house, Capel Hall, when he invited everyone from the club with their partners to a pre-season barbecue. He hired a band and it was a great do. In fact, it was a tradition that is still going strong. His nephew, Philip Hope-Cobbold, who is on the board, holds it every year at Glemham Hall, which he inherited when Mr Patrick died. It's typical Ipswich – they've always loved a party at the club.

"Anyway, Mr John loved my defensive partner, Allan Hunter, and the feeling was mutual. They were two of a kind, I would say, both a couple of rascals who loved a laugh. Mr John had three donkeys – Alka, Seltzer and their offspring Burp – and he suggested we should stage our own donkey derby. It was all hush-hush, nobody else knew about it, and we'd have preferred to have kept it that way. But the donkeys had other ideas.

"We got astride them but it was impossible to make them go the way we wanted. We could do nothing about it as they careered towards the back of the marquee where the band was playing. They just kept going and the next we knew we were all in a heap with Mr John almost draped over the drums. I remember Bobby Robson being very anxious for the chairman's welfare. 'For Christ's sake look after him Beat,' he said. With that, Big Al slung Mr John over his shoulder and we took him back to the house and upstairs to his room.

"We got him into his pyjamas but even then the fun wasn't over. Once his pyjama trousers were on Big Al tied knots in the bottom of them and, do you know, he turned up at the ground the next morning with them and asked who had done it. He couldn't remember a thing from the previous night – I think that was a familiar feeling to him!"

Beattie also recalled how delighted Mr John had been with Ipswich's 1-0 win over Real Madrid at Portman Road in September 1973, in the first leg of a UEFA Cup first round tie. The job was only half done at that stage – Town duly completed it a fortnight later with a tremendous goalless draw at the Bernabeu Stadium to send the Spanish giants crashing out of the competition – but Mr John was anxious to pass on his congratulations to Beattie & co.

"He wouldn't come into the dressing room immediately after the match because that wasn't his scene," remembered Beattie. "We had a day off and when I went in the following morning after training I saw him in the corridor, looking a bit apprehensive. He was trying to find the gaffer, Bobby Robson, to ask him if it would be okay to go in and say congratulations to the boys, but I just grabbed him and virtually dragged him in. You could tell he was a bit uncomfortable with it. The other lads were surprised to see him in there because it just never happened. His policy was always to avoid interfering in any way.

"He just blurted out a few words to say well done and while he was making his short speech Big Al whispered in my ear to get him into the area where we had the big bath. I was just a kid back then and did everything the big man said. The excuse I used was that some of the players were still in the bath and wouldn't have heard his kind words. He followed us through and without warning Big Al got hold of him and sent him flying into the water. He was fully clothed but he lapped it up and we were all in stitches. A few seconds later he asked for a fag and the three of us lit up. Then he calmly climbed out, walked out into the car park and asked his chauffeur to take him home. He was still laughing out loud as they drove off."

Another Ipswich legend, Scottish international John Wark, has good reason to remember 1981. Not only did he play his part in the club's memorable UEFA Cup success – the midfielder scored 14 times in the 12 ties and 36 goals in total as the club narrowly missed out on the domestic double of League Championship and FA Cup – but he was also crowned as the Professional Footballers' Association Player of the Year. He remains the only Ipswich player to win the ultimate individual accolade and recalled the night he was presented with the award at the

PFA's annual dinner, held at the London Hilton in Park Lane on March 15 1981.

Wark said, "We completely dominated the voting that year, with Frans Thijssen runner-up and Paul Mariner third, so you can imagine the party afterwards. I was sharing a room with PM, as I always did, so that was the venue and we must have had about 30 to 40 people in there, including a lot of players from other clubs that I knew.

"We just kept ordering and signing for more drinks. This guy kept arriving with another trolley-full of them. It was non-stop. From what I remember we didn't finish until about five o'clock in the morning and when we got up to get ready to depart the room was in a right mess with empties everywhere. But thankfully there was no damage – it was just untidy.

"When we got down to reception both PM and I knew we were going to face a large drinks bill so we checked how much money we had on us. I only had about a fiver and he had little more, so when the receptionist handed us the bill and it was for more than £400 – I think it was even closer to £500 – we were in a right old state.

"Just at that point Mr John arrived at the desk and asked, 'Is there a problem, boys?' We explained the situation and he simply said, 'Leave it to me, off you go.' He was taking care of it as we headed for the exit and just as we were going through the door he shouted to us with a big grin on his face, 'It must have been a hell of a party!' That was Mr John."

There was no finer ambassador for Ipswich Town Football Club than Mr John and every visitor to Portman Road departed richer for the experience, regardless of the result. Veteran BBC commentator John Motson, who attended a number of Town fixtures during his time at Culford School, Bury St Edmunds, said, "Coming to Portman Road will never be the same again without the humorous and welcoming figure of Mr John, but on a wider note neither will the game of football. He stood out as a genuine human being to whom the result of the last match or the next match was of no significance compared with the business of enjoying warm friendship and sharing spirited companionship. I am one of many whose life was made richer and whose job was made easier by the kindness of one of life's true gentlemen. I remember the club inviting me to be their guest at a dinner in London and meeting Mr John and his colleagues at the hotel where it was being held. We wandered into the bar and the grill was down, at which point a member of staff arrived to tell us the bar was closed but would open in about 15 minutes. Typical of Mr John, he replied, 'Can we have a drink while we wait?'"

Former local newspaper writer Eric Johnstone, now a senior journalist at the *Daily Star*, remembered an occasion when he was dispatched to London to cover a Southern Junior Floodlit Cup-tie between the youth sides of Ipswich Town and Queen's Park Rangers at the London club's Loftus Road ground. He recalled, "In those days the club allowed the local press to travel on the team coach for first-team, reserve and youth games. Bobby Robson, who was always very particular about allowing plenty of time for the journey, came along and so did Mr John. We arrived at Loftus Road well ahead of the kick-off. In fact, if I remember correctly we were the first ones there and the place had not even been unlocked. Mr John wasn't one for hanging around doing nothing so he suggested I accompanied him to the nearest pub. It wasn't the most exotic venue and the customers gave us an odd look or two as we entered. When they heard Mr John – in his country tweeds and with that posh accent of his – ask the much-tattooed landlord if he had any champagne the looks became even stranger. But the chap, who lived on the premises, replied, 'I've got one upstairs' and he went to fetch it. Mr John paid, we finished the bottle and we still made the kick-off.

"Champagne was once more the order of the night during Ron Atkinson's time as manager of Cambridge United. Again it was a youth cup-tie and yet again I accompanied the chairman to a pub across the road from the Abbey Stadium for a couple of liveners before the game. Ipswich won 3-2 with a brilliant last-minute goal from Alan Brazil and despite his team losing Big Ron cracked open a couple of bottles of bubbly, 'just because Mr John Cobbold is here.'

"Another occasion I remember was when he tipped me off that he had a big story for me and that I should make my way down to the ground. Eager to claim my exclusive, I wasted little time in turning up and was made very welcome. Mr John invited me into the boardroom, went to the drinks cabinet and brought out the port. It was some time later, by which stage we were both well oiled, that I suddenly remembered the purpose of my visit and asked him about the story he had for me. 'Ah yes,' he said. 'I am standing down as chairman and brother Patrick is taking over.' With all due respect to Mr John it was not the earth-shattering scoop for which I had hoped. But I suspect he knew that and just thought it would be a good idea if I joined him for a drink.

"Travelling with the team – and the Cobbolds – was an experience to remember. When Carlisle were in the old First Division in 1974 we travelled all the way to Cumbria by train, changing in London. When we reached the overnight hotel, and ventured to the bar for a pre-dinner drink, Mr John announced, 'I rang ahead from Euston and had three bottles of champagne put on ice.' We then sat down to dinner – two directors, manager Bobby Robson, coach Cyril Lea, physio Brian

Simpson and two Pressmen – and Mr John ordered six bottles of house white to accompany the meal!"

Another local journalist, Neal Manning, also recalled the same trip to Carlisle. He said, "We travelled by rail and after the game we called in at a hotel on our way to the railway station. Of course, the inevitable happened and by the time we took our seats on the train a number of us, John included, were quite merry. In his case, though, he had been drinking virtually all day and eventually he fell asleep. It was at this point that Allan Hunter, who was very close to him, decided to have a bit of fun. He took a serviette and wrote on it 'This man is a helpless drunk – please give generously' then he tied it round John's neck. He lay there for a while and one passenger even dropped a coin in his lap as he walked past.

"On another occasion we were down in Cardiff and I arranged for an old school pal of mine to call at our hotel on the day of the game. He got there just after 12 and I introduced him to John, who joined us for a few drinks. The two of them got on very well but when John invited him to join him at the match my friend said, 'No, that is very kind of you, but I tend to spend my Saturday afternoons drinking with friends.' John looked at him and replied, 'Well, what the fuck do you think I do on a Saturday afternoon?' My friend decided there was nothing for it but to take him up on his offer."

Dave Kindred, a former local newspaper photographer and picture editor, encountered the Cobbold brothers numerous times in the course of his duties – but one occasion in particular stands out ahead of all others. He said, "It was in 1976 when Mr John decided to step down as chairman and let Mr Patrick take over. It was pretty low key – a press release from the club and then the pair of them went off for lunch. The local BBC programme, *Look East*, decided that to help illustrate the story it would be nice to interview them and have some up-to-date footage of them, so they sent a film crew down from Norwich. They weren't looking for anything too elaborate, just a couple of questions and a shot of them shaking hands, but by the time they travelled down the A140 and tracked them down you can probably guess what sort of state they were in. They were half-cut and an interview was clearly out of the question. The BBC people didn't want to go back with nothing, however, so they went ahead and shot some footage. But because the pair of them knew there was no sound they started swearing at each other like a couple of troopers as they went through the motions. *Look East* broadcast it that night without sound and the presenter talking over the footage – it's called Out Of Vision (OOV) in the trade – but that was far from the end of it because in the days that followed they received tons of protests from various local Deaf Associations!"

Another local photographer, Owen Hines, travelled all over Europe covering Ipswich Town games and knew Mr John very well. Owen remembered the time he was sent to Portman Road when the club was formally opening its new-look indoor gymnasium after it had been given a makeover in the shape of state-of-the-art Astroturf flooring. Under the terms of the deal the manufacturers supplied the synthetic surface free of charge in return for the publicity they felt it was sure to generate via its association with one of the top English clubs. In order to maximise impact the club invited Fleet Street's leading journalists along with the familiar faces of the best-known BBC and ITV correspondents. To help ensure their attendance Town organised a five-a-side tournament on the new 'carpet' in which first team stars played alongside the journalists and the column inches and photographs that appeared in the following day's papers made the exercise extremely worthwhile. Owen recalled: "Bobby Robson was thrilled to bits with the deal and made it very obvious when he made a speech welcoming everyone. He extolled the virtues of the Astroturf, explaining it would enable the team to train no matter the weather and that it was a facility to make Ipswich the envy of all others. What he didn't realise, however, was that Mr John was up to his usual tricks. He had stopped en route to the ground at a local greengrocer and picked up a bag of mushrooms, which he then went and placed at irregular intervals on the gymnasium floor. Bobby was completely unaware of it until it was pointed out to him and he had no choice but to laugh along with everyone else as he looked down from the balcony and saw the 'damage'."

Mr John's nephew, David Paul, has many happy – and hilarious – memories of his uncle. From an early age he formed a close bond with him that remained until his death. David said, "I used to look forward to meeting Johnny. We would spend Christmas at Glemham and Granny was great, but Johnny was the life and soul of the party. I was only about 12 when he taught me to play backgammon, not an easy game to learn by any means and especially not when you are under the influence. We would be in the drawing room at Glemham and he would be drinking half bottles of champagne. He allowed me to have one – my parents knew nothing about it – and I had many delightful moments in his company.

"He was a great one for practical jokes. I remember him telling me one Sunday how he had played a joke on the Leeds United board of directors the previous day at Portman Road. As I understand it, they were predominantly Jewish, and as usual he invited them to lunch before the game. They accepted and it appealed to his sense of humour to have roast pork, crackling, apple sauce etc for the main course. He made a great fuss when it was being served – 'This looks lovely, can't wait to tuck in' – and apparently the looks on the faces of chairman Manny Cussins and his colleagues made it all worthwhile. After a couple of minutes the staff removed the pork and trimmings, which Johnny had arranged for them to do, and it was replaced by roast beef. Cue laughter from the Leeds people, who knew they'd been well and truly had!

"However, I remember one occasion when the joke rebounded on Johnny and he was very much the victim. The club installed some executive boxes in what is now the aptly-named Cobbold Stand and Johnny was keen to see what they were like. He decided to desert his seat in the directors' box for the very first time and sit, instead, in an executive box. Someone had convinced him that the glass had been darkened in such a way that while he could see out, those on the other side could not see in. When a policeman was walking round the pitch near to the box in which Johnny was seated he seized his chance and gave him a V-sign. Johnny started laughing but he was silenced when, to his utter dismay, the policeman calmly stuck two fingers up at the box and carried on his way. Then, once the shock of seeing what the policeman had done wore off, Johnny joined in with his companions as they laughed aloud."

David, now in his 50s, was also educated at Eton and he recalled that in 1982 he was farming in Denmark when he received a telephone call from his uncle. He said, "Johnny asked what I was doing the following Wednesday. He went on to explain that it was Bobby Robson's first game in charge of the England team and they were playing the Danes in Copenhagen. Bobby had invited the entire Ipswich board of directors as his guests but my uncle, Patrick, was ill and couldn't make it. Johnny said I could take his place and explained I would have to share a room with him. I should have been ploughing a field but this sounded a much more attractive option, so off I went to Copenhagen to meet Johnny and the other directors. We had rather a large lunch, as you can probably imagine, and later on Johnny surprised me when he said we would be sitting in the stand alongside the supporters. I said to him, 'You'll be fine, I'll look after you.' It wasn't new to me, as I'd been on the terraces before, but when we came out of the stadium there was a huge punch-up going on and I managed to get him out of the way. He was absolutely terrified. Not his scene at all. I remember I shared a room with him and he farted all night."

Mr John was far happier enjoying a drink with friends or, with brother Patrick a willing accomplice, playing a joke on some poor unsuspecting souls. Like the time the pair were staying at five-star London hotel Claridge's, whose website boasts: 'In the heart of Mayfair, Claridge's hotel is perfectly placed for the city, London's shopping districts and leafy Hyde Park. With award-winning service and business facilities, Claridge's luxury London hotel is a sumptuous retreat for the business traveller – or a luxurious indulgence if you want to spoil yourself or a loved one. Claridge's is a key part of London's history. Stars, socialites and the crowned heads of Europe have enjoyed this 5 star hotel for over 100 years. Some of the world's greatest designers have left their mark on Claridge's. Original features mingle with distinctly modern twists, refining the effortless Art Deco elegance that makes London's finest hotel so special. A stay at Claridge's is an unforgettable experience.'

It certainly was for John and Patrick's fellow guests, according to David, who added, "Johnny told me the story of how he and his brother created merry hell at Claridge's one night. It was normal practice for guests to leave their shoes outside their room last thing at night and to open the door first thing in the morning, whereupon they would find them polished to perfection. On this particular occasion John and Patrick had been drinking and before they retired at about two o'clock in the morning they moved from floor to floor switching the shoes around. This involved hundreds of pairs, not just a few. They had consumed a fair amount of alcohol but they still had their wits about them and took their own shoes indoors. You can imagine the scene the next morning. John and Patrick calmly left their rooms to go down for breakfast, chuckling merrily at the mayhem they had caused as fellow guests were flying up and down the stairs all screaming, 'Where are my bloody shoes?'"

David estimated that he spent 28 successive Christmases at Glemham Hall and remembered that in 1974, when he was in his last year at Eton, he accepted a challenge from his uncle. "Johnny said he would bet me 25 quid that I wouldn't make it – you know, pass my A-levels," he recalled. "Well, in the summer of 1975, I went off to find him and he was at the annual tennis tournament in Felixstowe. I told him I'd done it and he shook my hand, said, 'Well done' and wrote me a cheque for £25. I went off and bought a green double-breasted velvet suit. Wore it for years, I did.

"At that time in my life I appeared to have three choices – Army, university or something completely different. Well, I couldn't, or rather I wouldn't, join the Army. My exam results weren't good enough for university, so I went for the third option. I went off to London and did a 20-week course learning French. I found myself working for Prue Leith and some quite famous landscape gardeners in London for three years before I returned to farm in Suffolk."

Had things worked out differently, David may well have succeeded his uncles and other relatives by becoming a director of Ipswich Town. His father, Roger, a successful businessman in his own right, was offered a seat on the board by John and Patrick, only to decline. Had he accepted the invitation, following his death the position may well have passed to his son, as was the case when Willie Kerr resigned in July 1983 in favour of his son, John, who later became chairman before handing over to David Sheepshanks in 1995.

David often travelled to Ipswich away games in the company of his two uncles. He said, "I had a phone call from Johnny one day telling me to meet him at Ipswich Station and I thought 'Bloody marvellous' because I knew we were going to have a good time. Ipswich were playing in Southampton and after winning the game we made our way home. Johnny and I were in the company of two of the club's greatest-ever players, Allan Hunter and Kevin Beattie, on the train. We were smoking and drinking all the way home. That's how it was in those days but they are long gone. My uncles would turn up for the home games in their tweeds, plus fours and with their black Labradors. You know, they didn't really like football. Same with my grandfather, who started it all. He was into fishing, shooting and horse racing, but of course he was sold on the idea of professional football in Ipswich and vowed to make it happen. Johnny and Patrick carried on from there – they maybe weren't football fans in that sense of the word but they loved Ipswich Town. It was a bit like drinking – they weren't too keen on the beer that the family brewery turned out but they more than made up for it with other alcoholic refreshments.

"As a youngster I loved my visits to Glemham Hall. There was this very long table with Granny at one end and Johnny at the other. I always made sure I sat close to Johnny. He would tell some unbelievable jokes and because the table was so long Granny couldn't hear anything he said. My father was a bit straight-laced, I suppose, or at least that was how I saw him. But when we were at Glemham he would laugh out loud and I saw a whole new side to him. There was a tradition for attending church at Christmas and when I was about 12 I managed to get out of it. I was wandering round Glemham, thinking it was empty apart from me. I went into a bathroom and there was Johnny just about to have a bath. He threw a towel in front of himself and asked me what I was doing. Rather sheepishly I explained that I hadn't gone to church with the others. Well, he went on to explain that he never went either. It was just accepted by the rest of the family that he wouldn't be going along. After his bath we sat down and had a glass of champagne until the others returned from church. I was intrigued as to why he never went to church but I didn't have the gall to ask him why.

"To be honest Johnny was my hero. He made me laugh and I have some wonderful memories of our time together. He was a one-off. I remember after he died that Patrick invited my wife, Kate, and I to Glemham and I have never seen anyone so upset. He cried and cried at the loss of his brother. It was a very emotional time and Patrick was absolutely devastated, as we all were, that he had been taken from us at such a young age. I shudder to think what he would make of Ipswich Town now that it is under the jurisdiction of someone called Marcus Evans, who no-one sees. It couldn't be more different to the wonderful era when Johnny was chairman and the club earned its reputation as one of the friendliest – if not *the* friendliest – in the country."

One person who helped Ipswich to earn that reputation was Pat Godbold, who went to work at Portman Road 55 years ago and was secretary to every manager from Scott Duncan to George Burley. "What a debt of gratitude the cub owes the Cobbold family," she said. "Mr John was a joy to have around in his time as director and chairman. One day he popped into the old office, which was a Nissan hut, and asked me if I had ever seen a flying saucer. Then he told me to look out of the window on to the practice pitch. He went out into the middle with a dustbin lid and underneath he placed this rather large firework, which was pretty powerful. He lit it and I can still see him running away before the explosion. Within a few seconds there was an almighty bang and the lid flew high into the air. It came down with a real thump and he was laughing his head off. That lid never did fit the dustbin after that but he didn't care about that.

"He was an animal lover and he had a succession of dogs over the years. I remember him hearing that the Blue Cross charity in Felixstowe was seeking new homes for a Great Dane and a Chihuahua. He decided to adopt the Great Dane and he called it Thumper, which turned out to very appropriate. Soon after he got the dog he called in at the office and he was barely controlling it. I've never been a great dog-lover and I was quite afraid, but Mr John told me, 'You'll be okay, he doesn't eat human meat.' Sadly, some time later Mr John invited some friends to stay at Capel Hall and when they arrived they had their pet Chihuahua with them. It ran off into the house, where Thumper got hold of it in its mouth, banged it on the floor and killed it instantly.

"Years later, in Mr Robson's time as manager when we were starting to be very successful, one of the local television companies decided to make a documentary about the club. They were given permission by Mr John, who was chairman at the time, to film at his home, Capel Hall. They arrived to be greeted by him at the front door and he then said he would introduce them to the other members of the board. He escorted the TV people right the way through his house and out on to the terrace, whereupon he said, 'Here they are' and pointed to his two donkeys in the field. Mr John was always laughing and joking, and in all honesty the club was never the same again after he died. A big part of it died with him."